The Search for a Divinely Guided Life

A Spiritual Autobiographical Inquiry into the Experience of Divine Guidance

Mark Allan Kaplan, Ph.D.

The Search for a Divinely Guided Life:
A Spiritual Autobiographical Inquiry into
the Experience of Divine Guidance
(Previously Titled: Original Gravity)
Third Edition, Paperback
2014

© Mark Allan Kaplan, Ph.D.

Printed in the United States of America.

ISBN-13: 978-1500882730
ISBN-10: 1500882739

DEDICATED
IN LOVING MEMORY
TO MY MOTHER
LIBBY KAPLAN

Table of Contents

Acknowledgments	*vii*
My Search Through Time and Memory	*1*
Original Gravity	*4*
The Springs of First Grace	*11*
The Alley of the Unknown	11
The Hand of God	12
Celluloid Calling	13
The Hypnotic Frontier	14
The Creative Spirit	*16*
Creative Inspiration	16
Creative Vision	19
Creative Grace	21
Growing Orbits	*24*
The Shamanic Call	25
The Practice of Yoga	40
The Teachings of Christ	56
Many Paths, One Road	86
The Way of the Tao	87
The Sufi Path	89
On the Road with the Buddha	93
Journey through the Valley of the Shadow of Death	96
My Return to Judaism	101
The Remembered Gate	*109*
Notes	*111*
References	*115*

Acknowledgments

This journey of self-reflection has been a collaborative process between my self, the Divine, and all the beings that have graced my life.

I would like to gratefully acknowledge a few of my teachers whose wisdom, guidance and faith in me has been a source of personal growth and inspiration for me.

> Stella Adler, Elliot Aronson, Angeles Arrien, Hal Zina Bennett, Bruce Block, Robert Boyle, William Braud, Hedges Capers, Seymour Carter, Robert Churchill, Harvey Daniels, James Fadiman, John Firman, Jean Firstenberg, Rabbi Steven Fisdel, Robert Frager, Rabbi Judith HaLevy, Baba Hari Dass, Arthur Hastings, Louise Hay, John Heider, Gerald Jampolsky, Arthur Knight, Krishnamurti, Rabbi Shoni Labowitz, Frank Lawlis, Jill Mellick, Edward K. Milkis, Eric Morris, Barbara Myerhoff, Robert Nadeau, Lestor Novros, Father Seán ÓLaoire, Daniel Petrie, Asha Praver, Carol Proudfoot-Edgar, David Puttnam, Ram Dass, Rabbi Zalman Schachter-Shalomi, Sister Mary Ann Scofield, Rabbi Rami M. Shapiro, Ben Shed, Sam Shepard, Julian Silverman, John Soper, Kathleen Speeth, Brother David Steindl-Rast, Charles T. Tart, Jeremy Taylor, Antonio Vellani, King Vidor, Mark Waldman, Ken Wilber, Marianne Williamson, and Robert Wise.

I am deeply thankful for all the beings, known and unknown, of this world and of others, who have guided, assisted, and supported me through this process. I dedicate this journey to my family, my friends, and my teachers; and to all those who are seeking the Divine.

The Search for a Divinely Guided Life

A Spiritual Autobiographical Inquiry into the Experience of Divine Guidance

My Search Through Time and Memory

> I would like to pursue a search for God
> in time and memory.
> It is a search that will carry us
> on quests and journeys
> through life stories,
> through hells, purgatories, and heavens,
> through ages of life,
> through stories of God.
> – John Dunne [1]

In the spring of 1996 I was struggling to figure out the topic for my doctoral dissertation at the Institute of Transpersonal Psychology in Palo Alto, California. I had hit a brick wall in my mind and felt totally blocked. An old friend called and asked if my wife Sarah and I could meet up with him in Big Sur over the weekend. Needless to say I jumped at the chance to get out of the city and take a break from my internal struggle.

The next day we drove down the coast. The environment of Big Sur has always had a profound physical, emotional and spiritual effect on me, and this time was no different. As we entered the Big Sur area, tears came to my eyes and I felt as though I was returning to my sacred home. Suddenly, my mind opened up and I felt as though my thoughts were being cleansed by the whispering ocean air and the vast rippling blue sea. Mental boundaries previous held gave way to expansiveness. My mind became clear and my perception of my struggle to choose a dissertation topic suddenly shifted.

I realized that I was trying to think of a dissertation topic and approach that would fit in to the traditional model. I had lapsed into worrying about which topic would further my career, meet the requirements, be the most impressive, etc. Now, it was incredibly clear to me that I needed to find a dissertation topic that would be organic to my nature and process, and would continue my own personal growth journey.

Once this realization set in, my dissertation topic became crystal clear. My dissertation would become a deepening of the path of personal inquiry I was already on, my exploration of the experience of Divine guidance. For the rest of the day I moved and spoke in harmony with others and the Earth. Miracles happened, great and small, moment by blessed moment. And at the end of the day, I stood on the rocky shore of the cliffs of Esalen Institute, completely bathed in sweet and gentle joy. I felt a deep sense of gratitude as a certainty of purpose invaded my soul.

> I cannot doubt the existence of a guidance,
> which I dare to call divine
> - which can so invade one's soul as to set one's feet
> on wholly untried and unexpected paths.
> -*Joan Mary Fry*[2]

After returning to the city, I began my dissertation research into the experience of Divine guidance by reflecting on my own experiences of Divine guidance, utilizing a process called "spiritual autobiography."[3] This process uses the method of searching "...for God in time and memory"[4] through the exploration of one's own spiritual life experiences. This exploration takes the form of a spiritual autobiography in which we tell and explore the stories of our experiences of the Divine.

This methodology has arisen out of the field of *narrative theology*. Narrative theology is the study of theology as it is expressed in narrative form.⁵ The narrative or the story has been and continues to be one of the most essential means in which religious and spiritual values, ideals, and understanding is imparted and explored.⁶

Reflecting on one's own past experiences of divine contact is also believed to be an essential part of the process of learning to seek divine guidance.⁷ Within this process of spiritual autobiography, one also "passes over" from one's own story to the story of others and to the literature of the spirit.

> This is ultimately how he brings time to mind, how he searches through time and memory, for passing over avails him of the time and memory of others, and coming back leaves his own time and memory enriched. In this process he goes from man's time, the time of life stories, to God's time, the greater and encompassing time which is that of the stories of God, and he experiences companionship with God in time. He discovers in this the greater dimensions of man, those which reach beyond the self and the individual life story. And he discovers the face underlying all, that of the compassionate God and the compassionate Savior. (Dunne, 1967, p. xi)

The following is the story of my own journey of the spirit up to this moment in space and time. My journey has taken me through darkness and light, through great blessings and hardships, through encounters with spiritual beings and the literature of the spirit, and through my own story and the story of others.

Original Gravity

The journey,
though in one sense a hard pilgrimage,
up and out,
by the terraced moment
and the ten heavens to God,
in another is the inevitable rush of the roving comet
caught at last, to the central sun…
like gravitation,
it inevitably compels every spirit
to its own place.
- *Evelyn Underhill*[8]

I began my process of spiritual self-reflection by exploring a significant episode on my journey into the experience of seeking, receiving, and following divine guidance. It was the spring of 1985. I had just completed my graduate work at the American Film Institute. I was their new "Golden Boy." My graduate film, *Voice in Exile*,[9] was winning awards all over the world, and I found myself in a whirlwind of meetings with studio executives, agents, and producers.

During this time period, a friend of mine who had become a famous television star asked if I would house sit for him while he was on location in London for three months. The house was a beautiful wooded twenty-five-room estate in the foothills with a screening room, tennis court, swimming pool, gym, and rose garden. Within a matter of weeks, I went from being a struggling film student to a "hot property" with all the physical elements of fame and fortune.

One hot spring day I was sitting in a lounge chair by the pool of the estate talking to my agent on the cordless phone. We were discussing something we both knew was not true as though it was real. As our conversation unfolded, I sipped on a margarita and surveyed the lush landscape of the estate through my new hip mirrored sunglasses. Surrounding me was a manicured rock grotto with two swimming pools, a hot tub, and waterfall. A beautiful young woman I had just met was swimming in the pool. She smiled at me, blew me a kiss, and seductively moved her naked body through the glistening water.

Suddenly I felt totally empty. Everything felt like an illusion. I looked around me, and nothing seemed real. It was as if my life had become a Hollywood movie. My agent was telling me how great I was, and a woman I hardly knew looked at me with the eyes of an intimate lover. It seemed as though no one was really seeing me. They were seeing my talent, my title, the car I was driving, and the estate I was living in, but they were not seeing me. Then I realized I did not even know who I was.

Several weeks later I accepted an award in front of a large audience. I looked out at the sea of unknown faces. The sound of the applause danced around the emptiness I felt inside as I asked myself "What does it all mean?" That summer I put everything I owned in storage, bought a backpack, and boarded a plane for London in search of the meaning of life and love.

On my first day in London I met a sixty-year-old British postal worker in the Duke of Wellington Pub in Soho. He bought me a bottle of barley wine and told me it had a very good original gravity. I asked him what he meant by original gravity. He explained that it was the British method of expressing the strength of a beer. He winked and said I should always make sure I'm partaking of strong original gravity. As he spoke these words he seemed to momentarily transform from an intoxicated postal worker into a sparkling eyed mystic. In my mind, the phrase original gravity blossomed into a metaphor for living life to its fullest.

I spent the next three months backpacking through Europe. During my journey I started to notice myself falling into two distinct patterns of experience. One pattern seemed to consist of periods in which everything flowed smoothly. Things would unfold effortlessly and seemed to work out perfectly. I would meet people who would point me in the right direction where I would in turn meet others. I would have the sense that I was in the right place at the right time and that there was a grand intelligence guiding me. All the elements of my life and the life of those I met seemed to be in some kind of beautiful synchronized orbit held together by some strange unseen force … and life felt rich and full of "original gravity."

Then, suddenly, I would find myself in another pattern of experience. Everything seemed to go wrong, and I was out of the *flow*. I sensed that I was in the wrong place at the wrong time. Places I wanted to see would be closed or inaccessible. People seemed distant and cold. I felt isolated and alone. Every step was an effort, and I felt out of synch with everyone and everything.

Slowly I began to realize that there were certain thoughts and perceptions that seemed to precipitate and support these two different patterns of experience. A surrendering of my plans, expectations, and past memories preceded the periods in which I experienced a sense of flow and effortlessness. During these periods of flow I would tend to be totally in the present moment. I seemed to naturally accept things and people as they were. The periods in which I experienced everything being out of balance seemed to coincide with planning, expectations, and/or following a past idea, suggestion, or desire. A flood of past memories and future concerns also marked these times.

The qualities of my flow experiences are very similar to those described by Mihaly Csikszentmihalyi in his writings on flow.[10] These qualities include the loss of self-consciousness, a sense of being part of some greater entity, and an altered sense of time.[11] This experience of flow is "… like being carried away by a current, everything moving smoothly without effort."[12]

At first I tried to manipulate myself into having these flow experiences, but that only seemed to send me farther into the other experience. I began to see that each pattern of experience was related to the other. My periods of flow seemed to come from the surrender produced by the culmination of the frustration of the "out of the flow" experiences. I finally surrendered to the whole process.

I was riding on a train bound for the city of Rome. We stopped at the train station in Rome, and my mind began to blur. My body felt heavy and warm. My stomach was churning with tension. I felt a strange all-encompassing force holding me in my seat. An inner voice told me not to get off the train. This inner voice felt like it was coming from both a deep part of my own being and from beyond my self. I just sat there watching people get on and off. Then the train slowly pulled out of the station, and headed south out of the city to parts unknown. My head flooded with painful memories and fearful thoughts of the future.

Suddenly, all my regrets and worries seemed so trivial, and my mind fell into a deep emptiness. All my muscles went limp. I felt as though I was floating through the beautiful Italian countryside. Out the window were rows of beautiful tall trees with white washed trunks. Their branches were covered with tiny golden leaves that sparkled in the waning light. As the sun softly set over the rolling hills of old farms and ancient ruins, the past seemed to recede in the distance behind me. I thought of trying to find out where the train was headed, but the voice inside me said not to ask. It said to ride the train to its final stop. Suddenly, I felt free … released from my past and strangely at ease with the thought of heading to an unknown destination.

I rode the train till the end of the line, the town of Salerno. It was late at night as I walked out of the station onto the quiet city street. I walked across the street to a hotel where I could see a light on at the front desk. I knocked on the door. The young man at the desk let me in and gave me a room. The next morning I rode the bus down the Amalfi coast. I was enthralled by the scattered stone ruins, the sleepy villages nestled into the cliffs, and the beautiful clear blue ocean waters swirling into emerald coves of powerful jutting rocks. Along the way the driver would stop the bus and yell "hello" in Italian to some of the farmers working on the hills beside the road. As I watched people engaged in friendly conversations, I prayed to find some wonderful people to spend some time with.

The next day I met Bill and Diane, a middle-aged couple from San Diego. We started talking, and they invited me to come with them to the island of Capri. We spent the next few days exploring the island together, meeting fellow travelers, and having deep conversations about life. One afternoon, while Bill and I were talking about the trials and tribulations of romance we both suddenly realized that my last girlfriend in the States happened to be his estranged daughter. We both sat in awe of the unfathomable coincidence of our meeting.

Bill told me that he hadn't seen or heard from his daughter in years, and had been yearning to know if she was all right. Tears came to his eyes as I told him about his daughter, and his yearning was fulfilled. As he spoke about his memories of his daughter I received the gift of understanding more about her, and gained greater insight into our relationship. That night I sat alone looking up at the stars above Capri. I felt blessed by the gifts I had received, and in awe of the great mystery of my experiences. The rest of my journey was filled with miracles and blessings. I felt guided at every step by a loving and compassionate force beyond my comprehension. Though I had explored spirituality and caught glimpses of this force prior to my trip, none of my previous experiences compared with the combined depth, magnitude, duration, and everyday integration of my experiences in Europe.

When I returned from my trip overseas I was unable to retain my deep and continual connection with this force, yet somehow I felt as though I had awakened from a deep unknown sleep. Everything seemed different; old familiar people, places, and experiences had a different quality to them. It was as though my center of gravity had shifted.

> It is a disturbance of the equilibrium of the self, which results in the shifting of the field of consciousness from lower to higher levels, with a consequent removal of the centre of interest from the subject to an object now brought into view: the necessary beginning of any process of transcendence. (Underhill, 1961, p. 176)

Before my journey, my life was centered on career and finding romantic love, with short excursions into the realm of spirituality. After my experiences in Europe, the center of my life seemed to shift toward becoming the best human being I could become, and to find a way of reconnecting with the experience of divine guidance. I began to explore, more deeply and earnestly, the world's spiritual and religious systems for knowledge and practices that could aid in my journey. And ultimately, I was lead to this process of research and self-reflection, to deepen my quest to understand this strange and wondrous experience of Divine guidance.

When I surrender to a higher and deeper Source
Within and beyond my self
I transcend and include the different levels
Of my inner and outer life,
And enter into a glorious and miraculous
Kosmic dance,
Divinely guided,
In harmony with all that is within
And all that is without,
From the tiniest atom
To the greatest expanse of the universe,
I am held and impelled
By an original gravity,
A force of ancient origin
And of a continually unfolding newness,
Unique and original,
Universal and collective
And together,
You and I
And all of creation
Are balanced,
Integrated,
Connected,
And complete,
At home
In orbit
Around the sphere
Of all being-ness.

The Springs of First Grace

> Who moveth thee,
> if sense impel thee not?
> Moves thee a light,
> which in the heaven takes form,
> By self, or by a will
> that downward guides it.
> - *Dante Alighieri*

The next phase of my spiritual self-reflection process was to reflect back on my earliest memories of the sacred. As I explored these early experiences I realized that the tiny moments of grace and brief encounters with unknown forces from my youth were like seeds planted in the garden of future experience. I began to see that they were the "springs of first graces" and gentle calls to turn me toward the sacred.

> The basic interior measuring rod for discerning spirits is the whole history and shape of a person's relationship with God. This relationship must therefore be known by constant prayer and meditation and return to the springs of first graces. (Fleming, 1983, p.232)

The Alley of the Unknown

My earliest childhood memory is of a haunting mystical experience I had when I was in first grade. One morning, as I was getting ready to go to school, I experienced a deep sense of panic at the thought of returning to the ridicule and laughter I was receiving from my fellow classmates because of my stutter. Walking down the block with the other kids, the dread became unbearable. I turned the corner and slipped behind some tall bushes. As I watched the other kids going to school, I started to calm down. After a while, the street was empty. I slowly got up, turned down our back alley, and walked back to my house. I snuck into the garage, took my bicycle, and rode off feeling the urgency of escape. After riding through the neighborhood for a while, I turned down an alley and suddenly stopped.

Autumn leaves swirled around the cracked pavement of the alley, being blown in spiraling waves by the strong Chicago winds. White billowing clouds swiftly rolled across the bright blue sky above, and the electric power lines gently hummed around me. In an instant all my pains and fears vanished and I was filled with a sense of awe and wonder. Somehow I felt the power and beauty of nature washing over me and cleansing me. I sensed a presence of something vast and deep and unknown around me and within me. A feeling of safety and peace filled me, and I stood there for what seemed like hours.

The Hand of God

In keeping with the traditions of my religion of origin, Judaism, when I was thirteen years old, I graduated from Hebrew school and had my Bar Mitzvah. Throughout my years of Judaic studies after regular school and the various Jewish religious rituals I experienced, I felt no connection to the Divine, and actually grew more distant from the notion of a God. That summer, my family went to our summer home in Michigan as we always had done. One night, I went out with some of the older guys in our subdivision. One of the guys had a convertible, so we went cruising down the dark country roads, laughing and having a good time. I was sitting in the back seat with one of the older kids who was stoned on something.

All of a sudden, the guy driving the car swerved onto a side road, and stopped in the middle of the vast darkness of a wheat field. He pointed to the sky and whispered "check out the sky." We all looked up. I gasped as I took in the sight of the aurora borealis igniting the night sky with undulating rainbow waves of light. We all gazed in silence, in awe of the majesty above us. That feeling of a vast and unknown presence I felt years before in that wind-swept back alley returned, and filled me once again. I remember thinking to myself how strange it was to feel this presence in a back alley and a dark wheat field, and not in a house of worship. All of a sudden, the stoned guy started freaking out, screaming that it was the hand of God coming after us. At first we all thought it was funny, but then we soon realized he was really in a panic, so we tried to calm him down. We drove home, and I spent the next few hours alone, lying in the field behind our summer home, looking up at the hand of God, and bathing in its beauty.

Celluloid Calling

All through my childhood, I struggled with finding a way to communicate with others. My stutter made verbal communication difficult and emotionally painful, and I searched for others ways of expressing myself. I began to draw at an earlier age, studying at the Art Institute of Chicago between the ages of nine and eleven. Gradually expanding into painting, still photography, and architectural design; I received numerous awards for my work. When I was sixteen I took a film class in high school. I teamed up with a friend, and we made a super 8 film together for our final project titled *Progress*.[13]

I loved creating the film, and felt a sense of joy and purpose. When we showed the film in class, people laughed and cried. I felt a chill shoot up and down my spine as the flickering light and dancing celluloid images touched the hearts and minds of others. Time appeared to stand still, and I experienced a feeling of deep connection with everyone in the room. I also had a sense of great mystery, as though I had become a channel for something greater than myself. Suddenly, I knew that this was my path, my gift, my *calling*.

The Hypnotic Frontier

After years of unsuccessful speech therapy, my parents took me to a hypnotherapist during my senior year in high school. I remember my first visit to her office. After explaining hypnosis to me, she had me sit back in a large comfortable lounge chair. She dimmed the lights and told me to relax. Her voice was gentle and soft and very comforting. I closed my eyes and allowed myself to be guided by her words. Slowly I lost awareness of my body and the room around me, and was transported to an inner realm of memory, visions, and vast imagined landscapes. I remember feeling like I had stepped through a doorway into another reality.

After our session I was in an altered state. My body felt light, and everything around me seemed brand new. I was experiencing the sidewalks, trees, cars, and people with a clarity and calmness I had not known before. For a short time my mind was free of traumatic past memories and fears of the unknown future. The present moment filled me, and that sense of wonder and mystery I had touched before returned. During our sessions, I experienced what it felt like to speak without a stutter. While my fluency did not sustain itself outside of the hypnotic state, I got my first taste of the power and mystery of the human mind, and the vast frontier of consciousness.

I stopped going to the hypnotherapist when I went to away to college to study filmmaking at the University of Southern California (USC) in Los Angeles. In my freshman year, a fellow classmate took me to see Pat Collins, "The Hip Hypnotist," at her nightclub on Sunset Boulevard. The show was great, and I signed up for her classes in self-hypnosis. As I studied and practiced self-hypnosis, I gained the ability to enter the hypnotic state at will. I would often experience a sense of mystery and presence, and slowly became fascinated by this vivid alternative reality.

The Creative Spirit

> At the appointed time, necessities become ripe. That is the time when the Creative Spirit (which one can also designate as the Abstract Spirit) finds an avenue to the soul, later to other souls, and causes a yearning, an inner urge. (Kandinsky, 1977)

As a child I would draw pictures of other realms and futuristic worlds that would appear in my mind when I would look at a blank piece of paper. When I took up photography I found myself able to sense just the right instant to snap the picture in order to capture a human moment, natural phenomenon, or a certain spatial reality. Through my years of work and training in architecture I would have visions of architectural designs when I looked at a blank page or when I would pass by an empty plot of land. When I found my calling as a filmmaker in high school, the visions became even more pronounced. I would actually have moments when an entire visual story would play within my mind's eye.

Creative Inspiration

Through the years I have been creatively inspired by many things: a beautiful sunset, a tender human moment, a work of art, a song on the radio, a passing comment by a stranger or a passage in a book or newspaper. During my sophomore year of film school I received the creative inspiration for my film *Gun*,[14] while I was listening to the Beatles "Happiness is a

Warm Gun" on the stereo and reading a newspaper article about handgun violence. Suddenly, I saw a series of images in my mind's eye, which then unfolded into a series of stories. The rest of the story solidified when I rented a Magnum 44 prop gun and held it in my hand. I felt a powerful force inherent in the gun, which further inspired me to attempt to capture this presence on film. Throughout the entire process of making the film I felt guided by a creative spirit, receiving inspiration at each step along the way.

The word inspiration can be used to describe many things, including the drawing in of breath; a sudden brilliant, creative or timely idea; a creative influence or force that stimulates thoughts and/or ideas; or a divine influence or force that leads to wisdom, understanding, and/or revelation.[15] Besides being inspired to create, I have also had the experience of receiving inspiration in the form of seemingly divine influence and guidance from the creative expression of others.

One of these creative divine inspiration experiences happened to me at the Rijksmuseum in Amsterdam. I remember walking into the room where Rembrandt's *The Night Watch* was hung. I froze in my tracks and softly gasped (inspired). The painting's presence was so powerful that it felt as though I had entered the presence of some great force. The painting seemed alive, as though Rembrandt had captured the life energy of himself, the people he was painting and the presence of the divine, and fused it all into the paint and canvas. I sat in front of the paintings for hours, while it spoke to me through image, character, story, color and light about human struggle and divine yearnings within myself and within all of humanity. The messages I was receiving from the painting seemed to be answering some of the inner questions that had been on my mind just before I entered the museum. That night I lay in bed feeling a deep sense of gratitude for the gifts of the inspiration and guidance I had received at the foot of that giant wondrous canvas.

> Art is contemplation.
> It is the pleasure of the mind which searches into nature
> and which there divines the spirit
> of which Nature Herself is animated.
> - *Auguste Rodin*

Months later, I had a similar inspirational guidance experience at the foot of Michelangelo's "David" in Florence, Italy. Again, I felt a powerful presence in the work of art. Michelangelo and his David were alive in the stone. As I circled the towering figure, every angle revealed another emotional reality, from great courage to hidden fears. I spent the entire day with David; walking around him; sitting and gazing at him from different angles; and meandering through the gallery of Michelangelo's other sculptures.

At one point, I felt an inner prompting to go into the gallery by Michelangelo's unfinished sculptures. I followed my inner guidance and found myself in the middle of an art class. The instructor was explaining to the students that Michelangelo believed that each piece of stone had an image within it waiting to be released and that the Divine revealed these images to him and his job was merely to release them from their stone encasements.

> I saw the angel in the marble
> and carved until I set him free.
> - *Michelangelo Buonarroti*

The instructor went on to say that Michelangelo also felt that a work was complete when he had learned the lesson he needed to learn, so sometimes he would leave a piece physically unfinished because he was finished with it internally. This, he added was a blessing for humanity, because without these unfinished works we wouldn't understand how he created his masterpieces. Somehow, this information was exactly what I needed to hear in that moment. The lecture combined with the visceral experience of the sculptures gave me guidance for my life as an artist and my journey of the spirit.

Creative Vision

During my third year in film school I took a class in screenwriting and began to yearn for a great idea for a script. I tried and tried to think of a great and original story, but nothing seemed to come. One day I felt a strong inner urging to drive up to my favorite lookout spot on Mulholland drive. I followed this urge and ended up sitting all alone on a rock high above the LA basin. I closed my eyes, prayed for a vision, and made the commitment not leave that spot until I had received a great idea. The sounds of the city receded in my awareness and I immediately entered an altered state.

In my mind's eye I saw an entire movie unfold before me. It was unlike anything I had ever seen; a vision of the future in which humanity would take the next great leap in human evolution, an evolution of consciousness and of spirit. When the final scene played out in my mind I took a deep breath and felt a wave of gratitude. The sounds of the city re-entered my awareness and I opened my eyes. The sun was setting and its brilliant orange light was reflecting in the millions of glass windows in the valley before me, creating a sea of sparkling light. Tears streamed down my face as I looked at the majestic sight before me.

After my vision I went home and wrote pages and pages of notes, and decided to spend spring break writing the script. The next day a friend of mine called and asked if I wanted to stay in her condominium in La Jolla for a couple weeks while she was away during spring break. I smiled to myself and told her that would be great. When I got to my friends place I felt a strong desire to let go of everyday life and just immerse myself in the screenplay. I put away all the clocks and put the TV in the closet.

For the next two weeks I worked on the script while eating and sleeping when the spirit moved me. As I got into my own natural rhythm, miracles and synchronicities became common place in my daily life: I would go shopping when I felt moved to and ran into someone who I had been thinking about; I would be stuck on a certain section of the script, take a walk and then receive visions on how to proceed after being stimulated by a chance meeting with another person, or the words of a song on a radio, or some other seemingly common occurrence.

One day I was feeling blocked in my writing; there was a scene that just didn't seem right and I couldn't figure out what to do next. A wave of exhaustion hit me and I laid down on the bed and fell asleep in the middle of the day. I woke up at two in the morning and had a strong urge to walk on the beach. The moon was full and stars filled the night sky as I made my way down to the ocean. There was a strong warm wind blowing, and the closer I got to the beach the stronger the wind became. Finally, as I stood on the shore of the Pacific, the amazing sight of a powerful storm raging out at sea overwhelmed my senses. The wind was so strong I had to lean into it; bolts of lightning danced on the horizon beneath clouds pulsing with light; and the water churned with massive rollers that turned into giant sprays and crashing waves as they hit the rocky shore. My mind emptied of all thought and I stood in awe of nature's power and majesty. In that wondrous moment, the power and spirit of nature seemed to transform my consciousness and I received a powerful re-vision of the entire film that revealed the key to the rest of my story.

When I handed in my script I felt a deep sense of accomplishment; it felt as though the writing of this material was a gift in itself. Somehow I knew that this script would need to evolve over time and had faith that someday it would be made into a film. Over the years I have received additional visions and noticed that the story has become part of my own evolution of consciousness; my experiences of spirituality and consciousness over the years have translated into transformations in this growing screenplay; and as I write these new story elements I gain a deeper understanding of my own experiences.

Creative Grace

My first year of graduate school at the American Film Institute I experienced a different kind of creative guidance that came in the form of moments of grace; instead of dramatic inner visions, I found myself in a world that was guiding me through the creative process and speaking its story to me. This journey of creative grace began with a seminar with actor-playwright Sam Sheppard, who shared with us his process of writing stories by starting with a true-life event, character and/or emotional reality, and allowing the story to grow out of this human truth. This idea resonated with me and I began to search for a human truth to use as the seed for my next video project.

After weeks of searching my memory for a true-life event, character or emotional reality, I came up with nothing that sparked my interest. An old friend came to visit for the weekend and I put my search aside and just enjoyed her company. While we were dining at a restaurant in Malibu we had a weird and wonderful encounter with an old, seemingly insane vagrant who spoke to the empty seat across from him and instructed his invisible friend to "Write this down..." The statements that followed were at first bizarre and nonsensical, yet soon his murmurings became not only coherent, but, in fact, strangely profound. There was something about this man and his words that sparked a story that needed to be told.

As I began to write the story of *Write This Down*,[16] I had a series of synchronistic encounters with other homeless people who added to my story. Once the script was written, a strange magic, or grace, took hold of the entire production: The right people and resources showed up; the cast and crew entered a state of communal fusion; and the images and sounds that were captured were filled with a magical blend of powerful emotions, laughter, tears, madness and sacred truths. We all had the sense that the story was coming through us onto the screen...a story with a life all its own.

When we screened the video for the class the response was amazing. At first I thought it was a disaster because there was an incredibly long silence after the video was over. Everyone just sat there staring at the blank screen. Then, one by one people started to applaud and rise out of their seats, until I was the focal point of a powerful standing ovation. I noticed that tears were streaming from most of their eyes. I felt a wave of joy and then a profound sense that I had been an instrument of a force beyond me.

Years later, after my sojourn to Europe, I revisited the story of *Write This Down*[17] and turned it into a feature length screenplay with a writing partner. The creative grace returned in full force to guide us through the writing process. We walked the streets with the homeless, where destitute people came up to us and shared their stories; we would ask ourselves a question about the direction of the story and within a matter of minutes or hours the answer would come in the form of a phone call, a song on the radio or show on the TV, or a passing comment on the street. One time we created an additional character and asked the question if we had created a believable real life character. We took a walk around the block and there was the character we created with the exact haircut and clothes and behavior patterns.

Perhaps the most profound example of this creative grace process was the time my writing partner and I were sitting on a bench on the Venice boardwalk discussing a major concern we had about the fabric of our story which had unfolded into a world in which both suffering and wondrous miracles happened to the homeless, a world of deep despair and yet, a world of powerful spirit and grace. We were asking ourselves the question if this mix of grit and grace was a reality or just our imagined vision.

Just then a young homeless man with one leg hobbled up to us on crutches and asked us for a cigarette. We said we were sorry but we both didn't smoke. The man said: "Oh man, don't be sorry. I wish I didn't smoke, it's a killer." We offered him some change and he thanked us and continued: "You guys seem pretty cool. You want to hear something cool?" We said "sure." He smiled and said: "See these crutches, man, these brand new crutches. Well, yesterday I had a pair of old wooden crutches that were falling apart and I was freaking out and afraid they would break and I wouldn't be able to walk, man. Then I was on the beach, man, and there were these brand new aluminum crutches just lying in the sand with no one around." He stopped talking and looked around as if he was about to tell us a profound secret. Then he turned back toward us and leaned in close "God is cool, man, God is cool." With that he smiled and then hobbled away. My partner and I just looked at each other. We knew we had just received the answer to our question.

Growing Orbits

> I live my life
> in growing orbits,
> which move out
> over the things of the world.
> Perhaps I can never achieve the last,
> but that will be my attempt.
> I am circling around God,
> around the ancient tower,
> and I have been circling
> for a thousand years,
> and I still don't know
> if I am a falcon,
> or a storm,
> or a great song.
> - Rainer-Maria Rilke[18]

Over the years I have explored various religious, spiritual, and metaphysical traditions and practices. I have had many profound experiences and have encountered wondrous beings and realities as I sojourned through this mystical landscape. This journey began long before my trip to Europe, and has continued up to this very moment. Many of the experiences I have had during my pilgrimage through the landscape of the spirit have occurred in connection with the exploration of several traditions at once. For this reason, I will revisit some of my experiences in each segment, viewing them through the various lenses of each tradition.

The Shamanic Call

> We hear the lightning flash within our darkness.
> Then we see the thunder within this illumination.
> The one speaks quietly to us,
> and the other sings to us of our learning.
> Together they become one song.
> - Hyemeyohsts Storm[19]

It was the fall of 1979 and my junior year at the University of Southern California. Professor Barbara Myerhoff entered the classroom, and began to teach us about anthropology, myths, and dreams. As I listened to her impassioned call for us to explore our own lives through a process she called "Personal Anthropology,"[20] I felt as though someone had suddenly opened another window in my mind. My previous experiences with mystical realities, artistic visions, hypnosis, mind-altering drugs, and psychotherapy all came into greater perspective as I began to explore my own life and mind through journal writing, recording and analyzing my dreams, and unearthing my own personal myths and archetypes.

During this process, Professor Myerhoff introduced us to the world of the Shaman, the indigenous holy person. She explained to us that the shaman was the "expert of the injured soul"[21] who has been called on by the spirits to heal themselves and others. This *call* often came in the form of a sickness of which the *shaman-elect* would have to cure themselves with the aid of *helping spirits*.[22] Once they cured themselves by traveling between the waking world and the world of the spirits, they would have the ability to help others.

Professor Myerhoff then proceeded to initiate us into the shamanic path by passing out a small pouch to each of us. In the pouches were a small mirror, a feather and a quartz crystal. She told us that the mirror represented the underworld, the crystal represented the upper-world, and the feather represented magical flight. She then took out a drum and began to drum and chant a Native American shaman's song. A wonderful energy filled the room. My mind entered an altered state that seemed to be peaceful yet strong, gentle yet firm, and focused yet fluid.

After the class, Professor Myerhoff asked me to walk with her back to her office. She said she was moved by my personal journal entries about my stuttering, and asked how long I had been a stutterer. I told her how I had started to stutter at the age of three...My parents left me with my father's mother while they went to Florida to be with my mother's father who just suffered a stroke. My grandmother took me off the bottle, and told me if I didn't behave my parents would never come back. When they finally returned, I was stuttering.

I told Professor Myerhoff about my struggles to heal myself through speech therapy, hypnotherapy, self-hypnosis, and psychotherapy. She paused for a moment, and looked into my eyes. Her voice softened to almost a whisper as she told me that it was believed that stuttering or aphasia was one of the major afflictions that the spirits used to call someone to the shaman's path. Professor Myerhoff smiled, and told me that after reading my personal writings, getting to know me in person, and being deeply moved by my films, she thought I was being called to heal myself and to help others.[23]

At first I was just sort of numb. I thanked her for her insights as she went into her office. I walked around campus for a while in a daze and ended up in the courtyard of Mudd Hall of Philosophy, a place I often found myself when I needed to think and reflect. As I stared into the bubbling water of the circular fountain in the center of the gothic courtyard, my whole perception of my self began to shift. I had always seen my stuttering as this horrible and crippling handicap. Now, as I began to think of my stuttering as a challenge for change and growth from some higher or deeper source, a previously unknown heaviness seemed to lift from around my heart.

Sitting in the courtyard of Mudd Hall, and staring at the flowing waters of the fountain, I wondered if I truly was being called to some greater purpose through my stuttering and, if I was being called, who or what was calling me, and to what purpose. It had been a long time since I consciously entertained the notion of spirit or God. I had lost contact with Judaism years earlier because my experiences within the tradition had left me feeling empty and wounded. Now, years later, I found myself feeling that unknown presence or force I had experienced outside of my religious life calling me once again. As I explored the literature of shamanism assigned for our class, I began to get a stronger sense of this presence as spirit, and my notion of God opened up to include a subtler and more expansive view of the Divine.

> The spirit is everywhere. Sometimes it shows itself through an animal, a bird or some trees and hills. Sometimes it speaks from the Badlands, a stone, or even from the water ... Listen to the air. You can hear it, feel it, smell it, taste it. Woniya waken–the holy air–which renews all by its breath. Woniya, woniya waken–spirit, life, breath, renewal–it means all that. Woniya–we sit together, don't touch, but something is there; we feel it between us, as a presence...talk to it, talk to the rivers, to the lakes, to the winds as to our relatives. (Lame Deer & Erdoes, 1972, pp. 2; 108)

These words, from the autobiography of Native American shaman John Fire Lame Deer, deeply moved me and resonated with my own past experiences. They helped me to find a way of holding a concept of spirit that was both reassuring and inspiring, and inspired me to take my own *vision quest* over the Winter break.

After my fall semester classes ended, I packed a bag and got in my car and just started to drive. I felt drawn to drive into the mountains and ended up on the winding road into the Angeles National Forest. I reached the top of Mount Wilson and looked out on the Los Angeles Basin. Its distant rumble of civilization was enveloped in the crisp silence of the mountain peak, as all thought of my life in the world below faded from my mind. I was compelled to keep driving through the mountain high forest.

I ended up in Lake Arrowhead for the night and checked into a motel. After a walk on the shore of the lake at dusk, I returned to my room and began to read a book that Professor Myerhoff had recommended to the class, Carlos Castaneda's *The Teachings of Don Juan*.[24] I was instantly enthralled with this story of a young anthropology student meeting and being trained by a Yaqui medicine man named Don Juan.

For the next few weeks I was in an altered state, reading of Carlos' adventures while roaming through the mountain wilderness of Lake Arrowhead and Big Bear. I felt guided at every turn, and everything that happened seemed to be a message from spirit. The water, the rocks, the trees, and the animals, all had lessons for me to learn and were teaching me in their own way. It was as though I were seeing the world for the first time: The water spoke to me of fluidity; the rocks talked to me of stillness; the trees showed me how to stand firm while reaching high; and each animal had its own gift of how to be.

> Earth teach me stillness
> as the grasses are stilled with light.
> Earth teach me suffering
> as old stones suffer with memory.
> Earth teach me humility
> as blossoms are humble with beginning.

> Earth teach me caring
> as the mother who secures her young.
> Earth teach me courage
> as the tree which stands all alone.
> Earth teach me limitation
> as the ant which crawls on the ground.
> Earth teach me freedom
> as the eagle which soars in the sky.
> Earth teach me resignation
> as the leaves which die in fall.
> Earth teach me regeneration
> as the seed which rises in the spring.
> Earth teach me to forget myself
> as melted snow forgets its life.
> Earth teach me to remember kindness
> as dry fields weep with rain.
> - Ute Prayer[25]

One day, near the end of my journey, I was having breakfast in a café in Big Bear and felt guided to open the Castaneda book at random. I opened to a section that described how a warrior must make a friend of death, for it is death that can guide us in each moment to live life to its fullest.[26] Castaneda's words penetrated me in a profoundly deep way. I put down the book and suddenly became acutely aware that in an instant I could die. My awareness of my self and the café around me transformed and I felt an incredible lightness.

For the next few days I called on my awareness of death to guide me. It was amazing, all I had to do was bring the idea that the moment I was in could be my last, and I suddenly knew with certainty what I wanted and needed to do. I returned home feeling renewed and refreshed, and armed with a new and precious tool for guidance.

Inspired by my vision quest, my exposure to shamanism, and my experiences with Professor Myerhoff, I began to ask within for clarity about the direction and purpose that my stuttering was calling me toward. A while later, during a film project evaluation, one of my film professors said that he believed my stuttering had made me a great filmmaker. He explained that because words were so hard for me that I had found a way of speaking visually with great depth and power. Looking back at my life, I suddenly saw my creative endeavors into drawing, painting, architecture, still photography, and film as part of a great archetypal quest to communicate with others beyond the realm of the spoken word.

Not long after this encounter, I received the inspiration to create a dramatic film based on my own experiences and perceptions as a stutterer. The making of this film would be a shamanic-creative journey into the depths of my own psyche to uncover and share what it felt like to be a person who stutters. I sensed that the process of making this film could be healing for me and for others, and a culmination of my creative quest to communicate.

As I began to work on the story, the idea of creating a shamanic subplot emerged. The story would be about a young stutterer who would face his fears with the help of his grandfather, a retired anthropology professor specializing in shamanism. His journey would include the waking world, dreams, symbols, and archetypes. This film eventually became my graduate film, *Voice in Exile*.[27] Before taking on the making of this film, I worked hard to develop my filmmaking skills. During this time I explored the literature of shamanism, mythology, symbols, and archetypes, including the works of: Joseph Campbell, Carlos Castaneda, Michael Harner, Carl Jung, and Hyemeyohsts Storm.[28] Throughout this process I felt a strong sense of purpose and calling.

After graduating from USC, I attended the American Film Institute (AFI) to continue developing my craft, and to supply a creative container for the making of *Voice in Exile*.[29] During my first year at AFI, while preparing to begin writing the script for the film, I became very ill with a bacterial infection after eating a plate of seafood. I came down with a fever of 105, lost circulation in my hands and feet, and eventually lost consciousness.

While a friend tried to revive me, I felt my consciousness leave my body, and rise up toward the ceiling. I could see the whole room beneath me, and somehow was also able to see the entire house. As my consciousness floated above my body, all of the worries and concerns I had in life seemed to fall away like a shattered mirror. I felt calm and peaceful. I became aware of a powerful loving presence behind me. I had never felt anything like it before. In its gentle and all-encompassing embrace I felt truly alive, safe, and loved unconditionally.

I remember feeling a wave of surrender as I gave up any attachment to returning to or leaving the world. I saw my friend frantically looking for rubbing alcohol in the bathroom, and I thought to myself, "It is in the left-hand cabinet." Just then, as though hearing me, she looked in the left-hand cabinet, and found it. She ran back to my side, and began to rub my body. Slowly, I began to feel my body again. In an instant I was back in my body, opening my eyes, and looking out at the physical world once again. I looked up at my friend, and thanked her for her help. As I looked around the room I knew my life would never be the same again. I knew deep in my heart and without a doubt that a great and boundless Spirit truly existed.

I returned to my childhood home in Chicago, Illinois, and spent the next six months healing my body and writing the screenplay for *Voice in Exile*.[30] The familiar surroundings of my childhood aided in the unearthing of the emotional and psychological memories needed for the story. This entire process felt like a dream. As I descended into the darkness of my unconscious, the world around me seemed supportive and gentle. It felt as though the world was holding its breath while I journeyed within. A raven became the helping spirit in my story in parallel with my seeing large black crows following me wherever I would go. They seemed to be my helping spirits, both within my story and in my waking life, telling me I was on the right track.

After completing the script I returned to school, and began the process of making the film. This process was fraught with turbulence and confusion. Communication problems arose at every turn. My mind seemed to be waging a war between itself–part of me wanting to share my truths, and another part of me was terrified. When principal photography was finished, I was exhausted and burnt out. I went up to San Francisco to work with my composer on the score for the film, and he suggested I go to Esalen Institute in Big Sur for some rest.

Driving down the California coast was calming. I drove along the winding road south of Big Sur looking for Esalen, hoping that it would be before the spot where the coast road had been closed for the past year because of storm damage. Up ahead, I saw the signs announcing that the coast road was still closed. I stopped at the roadblock, and asked a construction worker when the road would be open. He smiled and said, "Right now, you're the first to get through." He waved and the crew lifted the barrier.

As I drove past the construction site I couldn't help feeling as though I were being divinely guided. I drove for a while, and finally found Esalen. Driving down the steep incline into the property, I felt an incredible sense of belonging. Even though I had never been there before, it seemed deeply familiar, like a long lost home. I went to the office and asked if they had any vacancies. They told me that I was lucky because there was only one opening left.

After checking in, I walked around the grounds in a daze, wondering what was happening to me. I found my way to the dining room, and sat at a small table by myself, eating my food, and surveying the colorful crowd. A middle aged Native American woman approached and asked if she could join me. I said sure. She smiled warmly and sat down.

Looking deeply into my eyes, she told me that she was a shaman and could tell that I had just been through a very powerful creative experience that was chaotic and painful. She continued, saying that communication was the central theme. At this point, I could only stare in dismay.

The woman proceeded to tell me that the creative endeavor was successful, despite the confusing nature of the experience. She told me I needed to replenish my energy by resting my body, following my intuition, and doing only what I felt like doing. Later that evening I floated in the mineral baths under the stars, wondering if my quest was of true value. In the darkness beside me, a man and woman were having a conversation. The woman stuttered as she told the man "… if you could only know how it feels." Tears came to my eyes as the hot water penetrated my pores.

Feeling rested and renewed, I returned to Los Angeles and finished the film. We premiered the film, and it was a great success. Stutterers and non-stutterers said they were deeply moved. The studios called me for private screenings, power lunches, and meetings. The film won many awards, and was shown at festivals across the country. Amidst all this, I was asked to show the film and speak at a national convention for stutterers. As I stood before the crowd of several hundred stutterers, I felt like the shaman who had gone on a journey to the spirit world, and was now bringing back a message to share with the tribe. I was truly overwhelmed by the response. Stutterers, their spouses, and their families expressed their gratitude for the healing the film brought into their lives.

I had been through patterns of experience that were similar to the shamanic rites of initiation.[31] I answered the call of my essential wound of stuttering by attempting the creation of *Voice in Exile*.[32] I experienced the dismemberment and renewal of the body, and the ascent to the sky and dialogue with the Spirit during my illness and out of body experience. I descended into the underworld of my unconscious mind through the writing and producing of the project. Throughout the process I conversed with the Great Spirit, the helping spirit of the crow, with a shamanic elder, and felt guided by unseen forces.

Finally I returned and shared my vision through the showing of the completed work. My creative vision quest was complete, yet it seemed as though my journey was just beginning. I thought I would feel whole and healed, but I felt empty and naked. All my fears were exposed to the light, the trappings of fame and fortune seemed hollow, and the person I thought I was seemed like an illusion. A few months later I found myself on the streets of Europe, continuing my journey to lands unknown and forces unseen.

> There is the entire world
> and everything in it
> that can teach you…
> There are the songs,
> the bibles,
> the cities,
> and the dreams.
> Everything upon the earth
> and in the Heavens
> is a mirror for the people.
> It is a total gift.
> - *Hyemeyohsts Storm*[33]

In the years following my return from my journey overseas, I felt drawn to take many excursions around the country, seeking out and exploring Native American sacred sites. I visited numerous indigenous holy sites, including Mount Shasta, Mount Rainer, the Black Hills, Sedona, Monument Valley, Canyon De Chelly, and the Hopi Mesa. The native peoples view the natural landscape as an integral part of their religious life because they believe it is both the container for human experience and that the earth itself is a living entity that offers physical and spiritual sustenance. Sacred sites are areas of the earth where the presence and power of the living earth is viewed as especially powerful and manifest, allowing heightened communication between spirit and matter.[34]

One of the first sacred sites I visited was Mount Shasta. During my visit to the Mount Shasta area, I continually felt as though the mountain was calling me. Its majestic rock face and the mystical circle of clouds that seemed to always hover around its peak seemed otherworldly somehow. One morning I knew I had to drive up the mountain, so I got in my camper van and drove up the winding mountain road towards its peak. About three quarters of the way up the mountain I felt a kind of magnetic field pulling toward a side road. I followed the force down the road and ended up in a grassy clearing. Across the clearing I could see several campers parked under some trees.

The magnetic force was calling me to drive across the field and park under a beautiful towering tree. I followed the guidance and found myself parked under the tree. A wave of exhaustion suddenly came over me and I had to lie down on the bed in the back. As I stretched out on my back I felt the bed, the van and the whole mountain start to spin. I fell into a deep sleep. In my dreams I found myself flying to other worlds, some beneath the mountain and some above the mountain in the clouds. These worlds were both ancient and futuristic, in a sense, timeless.

I woke up several hours later, feeling as though I had actually taken the dream journey physically. An inner voice told me to take a walk so I got out of the van and began to stroll across the grassy field. The magnetic force was calling toward a small mound at the edge of the clearing and I made my way there. I stopped at the foot of a large medicine wheel made out of large rocks and stones. Without a thought I walked in circles around the wheel and then reverently stepped into it and sat in the circle in its center. I shifted instantly into a deep meditative state and felt the mountain spinning again, but this time I was still and the whole universe was spinning around me. I suddenly realized that all the trials and tribulations of life that I had been experiencing prior to my journey were just minute momentary pieces of a vast ever-changing cosmos. That evening as I descended from the mountain, I felt lighter yet more grounded, and renewed in heart and spirit.

> The Medicine Wheel Circle is the Universe. It is change, life, death, birth and learning. This Great Circle is the lodge of our bodies, our minds, and our hearts. It is the cycle of all things that exists. The Circle is our Way of Touching, and of experiencing Harmony with every other thing around us. And for those who seek Understanding, the Circle is their Mirror. (Storm, 1972, p.14)

The following year, my wife Sarah and I were on a honeymoon tour of the country, when we made our way to the Hopi Mesa in Arizona. At first we couldn't find it. We would ask directions and then get lost, only to ask directions again. Finally we stopped at an old gas station in the middle of nowhere. The gas attendant was a very old Hopi man with a kind and radiant face. I asked him how to get to Old Oraibi, the central Hopi village on one of the three Hopi mesa's. For a moment he just looked into my eyes. I imagined that he was examining my soul to make sure I was worthy of entering the Hopi world. He slowly smiled, then told me that I was very close and that I should follow the signs. He pointed ahead and all of a sudden I could clearly see three mesas in the distance. I could swear they weren't there before, but I just figured I hadn't really looked closely enough.

Sarah and I thanked the old man and headed for the mesas. We drove up the road into the mesas and found our way to the edge of Old Oraibi. We got out of the van and began to walk into the ancient village. The houses were made of dried clay and seemed to rise up out of the high desert ground at the top of the mesa. Ahead of us we heard drums and chanting coming from a large crowd that filled the main dusty streets of the village. We met some other tourists who told us that we were in the middle of a Hopi rain dance. Sarah and I moved to a position where we could see the dancing, and watched with amazement.

Over to the side I noticed a couple of old men climbing down a wood ladder into a whole in the earth. I walked over and looked down and saw a group of old men around a fire. One of them looked up at me and for a moment our eyes met. I could feel his presence rise out of the hole and almost push me away. I moved away and looked out across the vast desert valley below. In the distance I saw dark clouds approaching. I stood mesmerized, watching the rain cross the valley toward the mesa as though the drums, chants, and dancing were calling it into being. The air around us became moist and charged with static electricity as the dance reached its peak. The drums stopped and the rain came down on our heads. I stood there in the rain, laughing, and feeling as though I had witnessed a miracle of communion between man and nature, each calling to the other and answering the call.

> The great sea has set me in motion and set me adrift,
> moving me like a weed in a river.
> The sky and strong wind
> have moved the spirit inside me
> till I am carried away,
> trembling with joy.
> - *Shaman's poem, Siberia*[35]

Several years later, after further explorations into spirit and deepening my quest for the Divine, I received another gift from the shamanic tradition. It was the spring of 1992, and I had returned to Esalen for an extended healing and work-scholar retreat. One evening, while participating in a Sanskrit chanting meditation, I started to feel feverish, exhausted, and achy. Closing my eyes, the sound of the chanting voices around me receded into the distance. In my mind I had a vivid vision of an ancient Esalen Indian village on the same ground as present day Esalen. I was one of the tribe.

Suddenly, I saw a Native American warrior with a spear charge out of the canyon up stream of the Esalen waterfall. A renegade tribe followed the warrior, as they emerged from the canyon and attacked us. At the end of the battle, we buried our dead under the very house I was chanting in now. We had a ceremony for them with fire and chanting. A medicine man led the ceremony, holding a sacred stick with abalone shells on it. At the end of the ceremony we threw the bodies of our enemies over the cliff. The medicine man put a medicine wheel in the canyon, and asked the spirits to protect us from any more invasions. He climbed onto the cliffs above the ocean, and carved a statue of a spirit out of the rock face.

I abruptly opened my eyes and tried to return to my present reality. I felt the hands of the dead reach up out of the floor and try to pull me down into the earth. The spirits told me that I should only be in this spot when it was my time to die, and they told me to meditate in the round meditation house above the waterfall. I slowly pulled myself up and left the chanting circle. Walking through the darkness of the clear night I tried to comprehend the experience. The next morning, after meditating in the round meditation house, I felt guided to go down to the beach and look for the statue on the cliff. I looked up and there it was, exactly as I had envisioned it (See figure below).

A chill went up my spine. Everything around me felt alive, as though there were a hundred eyes watching and a hundred voices whispering one ever-present call. The call of circling seagulls, the ocean mist, the sands beneath my feet, and the beating of my heart danced together in a strange and mysterious dance.

Esalen Cliff Statue

Everything that is, is alive
On a steep river bank there's a voice that speaks
I've seen the master of that voice
He bowed to me, I spoke to him
He answers all my questions
Everything that is, is alive
Little gray bird, little blue breast sings in a hollow bough
She calls her spirits dances, sings her shaman songs
Woodpecker on a tree that's his drum
He's got a drumming nose and the tree shakes,
cries out like a drum when the axe bites its side
All these things answer my call...
Everything that is, is alive
The lantern walks around
The walls of this house have tongues
Even this bowl has its own true home
The hides asleep in their bags were up talking all night
Antlers on the graves rise and circle the mounds
while the dead themselves get up
and go visit the living ones.
- *Shaman's poem, Chukchee tribe of Siberia*[36]

The Practice of Yoga

> Now hear the wisdom of Yoga.
> Armed with this understanding,
> you will shatter your karmic bonds.
> On this path no effort is wasted,
> no gain reversed;
> even a little of this practice
> will shelter you from great sorrow.
> - *Bhagavad Gita*[37]

I was introduced to the practice of Yoga years before my journey to Europe, while I was attempting to heal my bacterial infection. A friend recommended I try these Eastern physical exercises to aid in my recovery. The Yoga exercises were incredibly helpful in my healing process and also reduced my levels of stress and anxiety. I began to notice a shift in my consciousness on the days I started with Yoga. My mind seemed clearer and calmer and making decisions appeared to be effortless. One morning I was meditating after doing some Yoga postures and suddenly my consciousness floated out of my body. I seemed to be able to see the entire room around me. My perception extended beyond the walls to the entire house, and then out to the street. I saw people going to work and one man fixing his car.

My awareness returned to my body and I slowly ended my meditation. I felt an overwhelming sense of joy and peace. Out of curiosity I opened the curtains, looked out at the street, and saw the man fixing the car, exactly as I had seen him in my vision. For the rest of the day, I was in a very calm state. Whenever a decision had to be made I merely thought back to my connection with a consciousness that could see beyond immediate reality and felt a wave of faith and surrender. Then the decision would just naturally arise within me or from within the situation.

> After the mind has been cleared...of sensory obstacles, meditation furnishes a twofold proof of God. Ever-new joy is evidence of His existence, convincing to our very atoms. Also...one finds His instant guidance, His adequate response to every difficulty.
> - Sri Yukteswar (Yogananda, 1983, p.172)

After working with Yoga on this level for a while, several fellow Yoga students recommended I read *Autobiography of a Yogi* by Paramahansa Yogananda.[38] One day, during the pre-production of *Voice in Exile*,[39] I was driving along Sunset Boulevard and saw a beautiful public garden and lake. I felt drawn in, turning into the parking lot without thinking. Once inside, I strolled through the garden, and then stopped at the bookstore near the entrance.

To my surprise, I discovered that I was on the grounds of the Self-Realization Fellowship, the organization started by Paramahansa Yogananda. Without hesitation I bought a copy of his autobiography and went back home to start reading. As I read through the story of Yogananda's life, the matter of fact references he made to miraculous and non-ordinary experiences struck me deeply. It was as though the norm of his reality was a world of saints, mystics, other worldly beings, transcendent experiences, and everyday miracles and wonders; his was a world of divine communion with holy people, spirit beings and the source of all being; a world where every being and event in life was a divine encounter and source for guidance.[40]

> The stars are His eyes, the grass and trees are His hair, and the rivers are His blood stream. The ocean's roar, the skylark's song, the cry of the newborn babe, and all other sounds of creation are His voice. This is the personal

> God. The heartthrob behind all hearts is His pulsing cosmic energy. He is walking in mankind's twenty-six hundred million pairs of feet. He is working through all hands. It is the One Divine Consciousness that is manifesting through all brains. (Yogananda, 1957, p.25)

In the middle of reading Yogananda's book, a friend of mine called and confided in me that she just found out she could not have children. When I hung up the phone I felt a deep compassion for her suffering and wished there was something I could do to help her. I prayed for guidance and sat in silence. After a while, I felt guided to return to my reading. A chill rippled through my being as I read the next section of the book, which spoke about the healing of Yogananda's sisters' inability to walk and have children. After asking his guru to pray for his sister, Yogananda was told by his guru to return home and give his sister Nalini a pearl to help in her healing.

> A month later, her paralyzed legs were completely healed. Sister asked me to convey her heartfelt gratitude to my guru. He listened to the message in silence. But as I was taking my leave, he made a pregnant comment: "Your sister has been told by many doctors that she can never bear children. Assure her that within a few years she will give birth to two daughters." Some years later, to Nalini's joy, she bore a girl; and, in a few more years, another daughter. (Yogananda, 1983, p.272-273)

Suddenly I felt a presence fill the room, as though the soul of Yogananda leapt off the pages and penetrated my inner and outer being. I was guided to close the book and sit in stillness.

I had a vision of my friend being healed by a stream of light. Weeks later she called to tell me that she was pregnant. I was struck at once with a feeling of awe and a strange sense of fear. The next time I saw my friend I told her about my experience. She cried and thanked me for praying for her and said that she had felt a stream of warm light bathe her after our phone call. We hugged each other and sat in silence for a while.

After finishing Yogananda's autobiography I began to practice his method of yoga, called Kriya Yoga, which consisted of printed lessons that guided me in readings, affirmations, meditations, and energy practices.[41] Even though the practices were deeply moving, I found myself slowly drifting away from them and getting caught up in everyday living once again. I struggled between my desire for the Divine and my desires for the things of the world, and the things of the world were winning the battle.

After the premiere of *Voice in Exile*,[42] I was swept into the world of my dreams with all the trappings of fame and fortune. Yet, there was a growing emptiness inside of me as I sat in the plush offices of Hollywood studio executives and tried to figure out the unspoken political maneuvers of these rich and powerful people, and understand the unknown stirrings of my own heart and mind. I had reached the end of the rainbow of my dreams and found emptiness. My heart thirsted for truth, for the Divine.

> When you have an immense thirst for the Divine, when you will not give undue importance to anything else-the tests of the world or the tests of the body-then He will come. Remember, when your heart-call is intense, when you accept no excuse, then He will come. (Yogananda, 1957, p.41-42)

One day, in the spring of 1985, in the midst of 'running on empty' in the Hollywood 'fast line,' a friend of mine called up and told me about a Hindu holy man that was giving some talks in Ojai, California. I had an inner sense of being called to go and see this man. While my mind was skeptical about the whole concept of having a guru, my heart yearned for a true teacher to teach me the truth. The name of this Hindu holy man was Krishnamurti, and he was giving a series of discourses at an oak grove in Ojai, California. I bought two tickets to one of the discourses and asked a woman who I had been seeing romantically on and off for a while to come with me. To my surprise and delight she said yes.

The day of the discourse arrived and we drove up the coast to Ojai and made our way to the oak grove. We spread out our blanket under a tree and sat down amidst the hundreds of other beings who were there to see this man. Then there was a hush in the grove and all eyes shifted toward the stage as a thin, elderly man slowly glided across the stage with the agility of a young man and sat down on a stool. His body seemed to instantly and completely relax as he looked out at the crowd in silence. Being in his presence was a powerful experience and I entered an altered state of consciousness the moment he had entered the grove. As he began to talk his words seemed to penetrate right through me, and I had the sense that his voice was coming from beyond the thin veil of his physical body.

> We are going to talk over together the whole question of pleasure, sorrow, death, and what is it that human beings throughout the world have sought beyond the physical, daily, troublesome, boring, lonely life. What is there beyond, not only for the individual, but for the whole of humanity? What is there that is not

> touched by thought; that has no name; that may be eternal, everlasting and enduring? (Krishnamurti, public discourse, 1985)

For the next hour and a half I sat mesmerized by his presence and his words. I felt as though I was in the presence of a totally different kind of human being. I had never experienced a person like this. His presence filled the grove and penetrated deep into my soul, and I could almost feel the voice of the Divine channeling through the body of this being. For a moment I thought that I had found my guru, but in that moment he told us he was not a guru and that the true guru was in each of us.

> Let us consider our relationship with each other, now, between you and the speaker, that relationship is very important to understand. He is not persuading you to any point of view; he is not putting any kind of pressure so that you listen, accept or deny. He has no authority; He is not a guru. (Krishnamurti, public discourse, 1985)

I listened with deep rapture, as Krishnamurti seemed to talk directly to me, explaining why I had been feeling so empty in the world of fame, fortune, success, failure, and the pleasures of the senses. Like a thirsty wanderer in a barren desert who had just come to an oasis, I drank his every word, and experienced a great witnessing of my life. I had asked in my heart for an answer to my confusion, and I received it on that gentle spring day in the shady Ojai oak grove. I saw that I was at the crossroads of the two ways of life that the great Hindu Upanishads speak of:

> ...an ignorant, narrow, selfish way of life which seeks temporary, unsatisfying, unreal ends; and a way of life which seeks to relate itself to the Supreme Reality of the universe, so as to escape from the needless misery of ordinary existence into undying bliss. (Hume, 1971, p. vii)

After Krishnamurti finished his discourse and left the stage, I sat in silence next to the woman who came with me. All the turbulent thoughts I had had about our on and off romantic relationship and my experiences in Hollywood left my mind, and I found myself in a wondrous state of stillness. We looked into each other's eyes, and for a brief moment in time all of our barriers to each other and ourselves were gone. We were experiencing the state of love that Krishnamurti had spoken of during his talk.

> What is love...is it sensation, sexual? ...Is love pleasure? ...Is love desire, is love thought, is love something that you hold or possess? ...When one realizes all that is not love: Pleasure, sensation...desire...fear...hate; ...if we could truly negate what is not love, ...totally put aside entirely all that is not love, ...then that perfume is there...then there is love... (Krishnamurti, public discourse, 1985)

We drove back to Los Angeles and spent the weekend in a state of shared bliss at the beautiful estate that I was taking care of at the time. All the fear and hesitations between us were gone; we moved as one, guided by a field of all-encompassing love. At the end of the weekend, our fears returned and we once again found ourselves back in our tortured relationship. In the weeks to come the anxiety and emptiness I had been feeling prior to Krishnamurti's talk came back to me with an even greater force. I became increasingly aware of the illusory quality of the world of fame and fortune. I had received a greater understanding of the situation I was in but I was still uncertain about how to proceed. I found myself surrounded by the trappings of fame and fortune, a beautiful estate, fancy cars, and a high-powered agent. I had beautiful women fawning over me while the one I loved was running away. All of it felt illusory, and I prayed for a sign to show me the way.

A week later, another friend of mine called and asked if we could have lunch. He said he had something important to discuss with me. At the lunch, my friend told me that he sensed I was lost inside and that he felt I needed to get away for a while. He suggested I go to Europe and broaden my experience of life. His words rang true within me and I felt a weight lift off of me. I knew with a strange certainty that this was the direction I had been seeking. After that everything fell into place, and within a few months I found myself on the streets of Europe exploring new worlds, and experiencing myself without the constructs created by personal trauma, family, and culture. Krishnamurti's words followed me on my journey as I lived out some of the lessons given to me on that day in Ojai.

I remembered his words about love as I was challenged to peel away all that was not love within me; and I remembered his words about beauty as I struggled to peel away all that stood between myself and the beauty all around me. As I sat on a train entering Paris and watched the full moon setting in one window and the glowing sun rising in another I realized that my first response to beauty was to look at it as a filmmaker, divining the perfect shot, and then to look at it through the lens of all my past experiences. But in that moment it all melted away and I experienced true beauty once again.

> What is beauty? Is it in the mountains; in the shadows; in the dapple light under these trees? Is it a sheet of water still in the moonlight or the stars of a clear evening; or the beautiful face...well proportioned? Or does it lie in the museums, the pictures, the statues? ...So what is beauty? ...Is not beauty something that takes place when you are not? When you, with all your problems, with your anxieties, insecurity, whether you are loved or not loved, when you with all the psychological complexities are not, then that state is beauty. (Krishnamurti, public discourse, 1985)

Months later, after hundreds of wondrous moments of beauty, I found myself on the island of Capri off the coast of Italy. The husband of the couple who owned the bed and breakfast I was staying at was also a fisherman named Alfredo. He was a simple, happy and joyous man; and one day I asked him his secret. Alfredo laughed and said he would have to show me. He led me out of the bed and breakfast and took me with him to pick wild dandelions on a hilltop above the island. We stopped and looked out at the beautiful vista.

Alfredo looked at me and said "Many powerful people come to this island, from your country, from my country, from many countries, and they rent my boat. But most of them don't see my boat, they don't see the ocean, they don't see this beauty." Pointing to his wrist to signify a wristwatch and then rubbing his fingers together to represent money he continued, "…all they see is this and this, time and money, time and money, they don't see anything else. This is very sad; they are very poor; I am very rich; look at what I have."

Opening his arms to the beauty around us Alfredo began to sing and then continued to pick dandelions. I felt a chill move up my spine as his words, so similar to Krishnamurti's, resonated within me; and a sense of being divinely guided to this moment swept through my soul. Alfredo stopped and turned and told me, "Remember, the last shirt has no pockets!"

The next day, two American girls came to the Bed and Breakfast and Alfredo made sure that the three of us sat together at the breakfast table. He whispered to me once again "...the last shirt has no pockets." I laughed and enjoyed their company. The lessons of my journey came together in my entire being and for the rest of my trip I was able to follow in the way of both Alfredo and Krishnamurti, being fully present to love and beauty. Near the end of my European adventure, I returned to Paris and met a young woman from Vancouver, Canada. I was able to effortlessly be in a state of love without all my fears and neuroses, and we had a miraculous affair in Paris, swimming in a sea of love and beauty.

I found that when I was in that state of love, when all that is not love ceases to be, and that state of beauty, when I allowed myself to dissolve into what is beauty, everything seemed to be divinely guided; there was no need to seek it, it was just there moving me like the sun moves the planets. My journey from the New World of Hollywood to the Old World of Hindu thought and the wonders of Europe taught me that the guidance, love, and beauty I was seeking was already there and all I needed to do was remove the obstacles within myself...

> It is there when you negate everything that is not...it is an immense thing to come upon...nothing can give it to you, but if in your being you put aside all that which is not...when you with all your problems are totally empty, then the other thing exists (Krishnamurti, Public Discourse, 1985).

When I returned home from Europe, I went back to Hollywood and continued my struggles between success and failure, love and despair, and truth and illusion. A friend of mine from India told me about a Himalayan yogi named Baba Hari Dass who had an Ashram in Northern California where he taught *Ashtanga* Yoga, which is a form of Raja or Royal Yoga that includes the eight limbs or parts (Ashtanga) of the yogic practices described by the ancient Yogic sage Patanjali in his *Yoga Sutras*.[43] The eight limbs of Ashtanga Yogic practice are: Restraints, observances, posture, breath control, withdrawal of sense perception, concentration, meditation, and superconsciousness.[44] After hearing all about Hari Dass and his ashram, I went up for a weekend Yoga intensive with both anticipation and apprehension.

On the first night, we all sat on the floor in the community room after dinner and waited for Baba Hari Dass to enter. After an introduction by one of the instructors, Hari Dass came into the room and sat down in the front. He had a twinkle in his eye and a gentle presence. For a moment, he seemed to look directly into my eyes. In that moment I felt him look right through me. I wondered if we were really connecting on this level. Then he smiled and nodded as though he heard my question, before he turned away and gave his attention to the questions of the group.

Having observed a vow of silence for many years, Baba Hari Dass answered the questions by writing on a small chalkboard and having an assistant read them out loud. That night I didn't ask any questions; I didn't have to because every question I wanted to ask was answered before I could raise my hand. Later I would learn that this form of psychic communication and guidance between Guru and disciple is considered common.[45]

> As the psychic tie between teacher and disciple grows stronger, we sense that the teacher knows us fully and witnesses our thoughts

and actions. We sense that our spiritual teacher is very close to us, recognizes our soul, and is familiar with our inner thoughts and feelings. (Bogart, 1997, p.131)

That weekend I immersed myself in the many varied practices of body, mind, heart and spirit that comprise the system of Ashtanga Yoga and began my many years of study and training with Baba Hari Dass. During one of a series of training intensives I had a deeply penetrating experience. It was the end of a long day of yoga practice and I was lying in bed, slowly approaching the first stage of sleep. Suddenly I felt a jolt of energy in the base of my spine. It shot up my spine like a bolt of lightning. My upper body was lifted off the bed, bending at the waist. My perception of this movement was strange, as though I perceived the experience in the past, present, and future all at the same time. Once my body was sitting up in bed, the bolt hit my heart, twisting my torso upward and to the left. In a moment, it was gone. My body was tingling all over and flushed with waves of heat.

In the morning I had a private session with Baba Hari Dass. He asked me several questions about the experience and then asked for my date of birth. Hari Dass stared into my eyes for several minutes then he opened an old sacred text and appeared to be looking up some kind of secret code. He told me that I had a *Kundalini* experience and that the energy was a form of divine guidance, telling me that I needed to do emotional or heart work, because fear was blocking my ability to love. He recommended that I expand my practice into the way of *Bhakti*, the path of devotion and love.[46] We then talked about my continuing struggle between the world of the senses and the world of the spirit. Hari Dass then told me I had many fears that I needed to face and gave me a Hindu name to help me with my journey; this name was Ranjit, the one who wins the battles.

Over the next few years I battled the illusions of Hollywood and myself, and continued my spiritual work. During this time I met another teacher on the path of Yoga, Ram Dass. Through the experiences of several in-person discourses, listening to his tapes, and reading his books, Ram Dass taught me how to hold a serious devotion for practice while also allowing feelings of joy and a lightness of being. This lightness of being is a way of holding whatever happens as "grist for the mill."[47] This perspective helped me to be open to guidance everywhere I looked, recognizing that it is "… all God in drag."[48]

On the first day of a weekend intensive in Los Angeles in the spring of 1991, I was standing in the lobby of the auditorium, waiting for Ram Dass with the rest of the crowd of seekers. I saw Ram Dass working his way through the crowd and struggled with my egos desire to be noticed as a special person. Just then, Ram Dass stopped in front of me, looked into my eyes and smiled. All my thoughts shattered into silence as we stared into each other's eyes. For a brief moment, time stood still and the sounds and sensations of the crowd around us receded into the distance as I received Darshan from Ram Dass.

> Darshan literally means a gaze or a look. Thus, it means having a look at the teacher. It is also the time when the teacher has a look at us and when we may receive the teacher's glance - which can be a conduit for direct transmission of the teacher's love, power, and awakened consciousness. (Bogart, 1997, p.86)

My thoughts of specialness returned after a while and I shattered the moment of deep connection as I got caught in introducing myself to Ram Dass. He politely shook my hand, gave a little giggle, and proceeded on his way. As he walked away I became sharply aware of receiving a great lesson. I let my ego thoughts fall away once again and followed the crowd into the room in a state of heightened awareness and bliss.

The next morning Ram Dass announced that he had had three thousand wrist malas, bracelets of sacred beads used in meditation practice, handmade in India and brought them back as a gift for each of us. They were made from tulsi wood, which is the sacred wood of Ram. Each mala had a thread from Ram Dass's guru's blanket. Ram Dass joked about having a moment of spiritual materialism and then proceeded to hand them out. People made several lines, and many of us struggled between being spiritually patient and materialistically impatient. When it was my turn to approach Ram Dass and receive the gift, a woman in the line next to me rushed in front of me. For a split second I thought of fighting for "my" place in line, but then I experienced a moment of peaceful detachment and gently let the woman proceed. Ram Dass looked at me and smiled knowingly, cupping the mala intended for me in his hand and saving it for me. Several other people rushed in front of me, and I just patiently waited.

During this time I felt that Ram Dass and I were in psychic communication and I totally surrendered into the situation. Within my consciousness, I experienced a veil being pulled back revealing my thoughts of specialness and attachment to material objects. I was able to witness them as though they were separate from who I really was. Then there was a moment of stillness and Ram Dass looked at me and nodded for me to approach. I walked up to him and received the gift of the mala beads with a sense of detached gratitude. Holding the beads in my hand, I could feel a transfer of energy taking place. The warmth of the beads radiated in my hand and I perceived two sets of beads, one material and one ethereal. I whispered a simple thank you as a feeling of being blessed washed over me. I felt blessed for the gift of the mala beads, and for the subtle, seemingly psychic guidance I received in the lobby and standing in the mala line.

Once we all got the mala beads, Ram Dass lead us through a group chant using the beads. We chanted the Sanskrit mantra, "Aditya Hridayam Punyam, Sarv Shatru Beena Shenam," which can be translated as "All darkness vanishes from life for those who keep the sun in their heart."[49] Half way through the chant I stopped doing the chant and the chant started to do me. By the time the chant was over I indeed felt the sun shining in my heart. I entered a gentle state of bliss that stayed with me throughout the weekend in varying degrees of depth and duration. I felt a divine presence and grace within me and around me, as some of the veils of my thoughts were swept away once again and I entered a state of no longer seeking, but just being.

> The presence and the grace is here, the awakening is out of the veil of the mind that kept you from acknowledging it...God's always here, it's not like 'God come to me,' its let me have my veil thinned so I can recognize the grace. All of that, the concept of a presence and something that elicits grace is all within what is called dualism, meaning your separate and your relating to something and then in the process of relating, the veils disappear and then you realize there was no separateness. The realization is of the oneness that is behind the two. So, to the extent that you think that you are a seeker on a journey going somewhere, to that extent, God's presence and grace is still separate from you. The minute you die as the seeker, God's presence is. Which is all there was anyway. You were just busy being separate. (Ram Dass, 1991)[50]

The following year, my explorations into the literature and practices of Yoga and Hinduism culminated in a powerful experience that seemed to embody all my learning. While on my healing and work-study retreat at Esalen in the spring of 1992, I experienced a synthesis of my yogic practices. My workgroup gathered together for movement meditation sessions every morning for a month. During these sessions I suddenly started to perform my yoga postures in a fluid dance-like form. Each posture flowed into the next. My movement and breath flowed together and combined with the music, creating a process that was beyond what I had experienced before. I felt as though an unseen force was guiding my movements. I moved without effort and my mind became still and peaceful.

These experiences occurred every morning for the whole month and became progressively more profound. Finally, on the last day of our sessions, a few days after my shamanic vision during the Sanskrit chanting meditation, I finished my yogic dance and entered a deep altered state of consciousness that was similar to Underhill's concept of the mystical state of communion, in which one experiences a sort of spiritual marriage of one's soul with the Divine.[51]

For the rest of that day I walked around Esalen in a state of bliss. I felt one with everyone and everything around me. I moved around as though I was a wave in an ocean, being guided by an unseen current. I would think of someone and they would appear. I would turn a corner and be in the right place at the right time. My heart seemed to open like a flower, and a feeling of unconditional love emanated from within me and penetrated me from all directions. At the end of the day my state of bliss dissolved as thoughts of fear entered into my conscious mind. The more I tried to hold onto the state of consciousness, the more it dissipated.

Some of the elements of this experience were similar to those I had encountered on my trip to Europe and in brief moments on my spiritual journey, but in a more heightened and concentrated form. I had returned to the state of divine flow I had experienced before, but this time I achieved a much more profound and deeper state. For twelve hours I felt as though I had crashed through all the veils of illusion and become one with the true nature of things that the Yogic literature speaks of:

> The unreal hath no being;
> the real never ceaseth to be;
> the truth about both
> hath been perceived by the seers
> of the Essence of things.
> - Bhagavad-Gita[52]

The Teachings of Christ

> He gathereth into his Spirit,
> and he teacheth those that abide in his Spirit,
> and giveth unto them eternal life,
> eternal virtue,
> eternal nourishment,
> in and from his Spirit.
> - Isaac Penington[53]

On my journey through Europe I noticed that at the center of most of the towns and villages stood an old church. Every hour, the church bells rang out and echoed down the centuries old streets. Gradually I became drawn to these churches and would spend many hours basking in their awe inspiring architectural and spiritual environment. Whenever I found myself out of the flow of things I would go to the church and inevitably its sacred atmosphere would miraculously shift my state of consciousness and bring me back into the divine flow experience.

Sometimes it was the prayer services that moved me; at other times it was the celestial voices of the choir; yet even when I just sat in the silence of an empty church, something wondrous washed through me. It felt as though centuries of ritual and prayer had mixed with the Divine Presence and become a living companion to the brick, mortar, wood, and glass. Often, when I would leave a church, I would wander the streets in a flow state and receive synchronistic gifts of guidance. Sometimes these synchronistic gifts of guidance would turn into a chain of synchronicities leading me through a series of wondrous experiences and encounters.

One such series of events began in Vienna, Austria. I had been in Vienna for a few days and was experiencing an extreme state of disharmony. I was lost in despair, reflecting on lost loves and missed opportunities in my life. One day I visited the home of Sigmund Freud and my inner turmoil seemed to increase as I walked through the dimly lit rooms of the historic apartment. Afterward I walked around the streets of Vienna. It was a cool and gray fall day. I ended up at St. Stephan's Cathedral in the center of town. The cathedral was unusually deserted and I took a seat in the rear of it cavernous main sanctuary. Tears welled up in my eyes as my inner struggle came to a head. Something inside me snapped and I felt an intense feeling of surrender. I prayed to God and asked for help. A wave of stillness moved through me and for several minutes I sat in a silence that permeated the space within me and all around me.

A group of tourists entered the cathedral and I had a strong inner prompting to leave the building. I followed the inner guidance, which led me out of the building, through the central plaza and down a street I hadn't been on before. I meandered through the streets, following my inner promptings of what direction to take. Finally I stopped by a beautiful park and sat on a bench. I had no idea where I was or how to get home. For a moment I panicked. Then an inner voice assured me I would be okay. Just then a middle-aged man with dark hair sat down next to me and said hello. He recognized me from the pension we were both staying at and he struck up a conversation. He told me he was a psychologist from Los Angeles on his way to Nepal for an extended spiritual retreat. We ended up talking for hours about our personal struggles between worldly and spiritual drives within us. Our conversation felt like an answer to my prayer, giving me insight into the inner turmoil I had been going through. We walked back to the pension together and had dinner at a nearby café.

The following morning, while we were both checking out of the pension, the man gave me a copy of book *Narcissus and Goldmund* by Hermann Hesse[54] and told me that he thought it might be helpful for my struggle. I thanked him; we hugged and went our separate ways. I went to the train station and got on the first train heading west. I found a nice window seat, took out the book, and began to read it. I instantly became enthralled in the books fictional story of two medieval Christian men struggling between the monastic and worldly paths of life. The story seemed to speak directly to my inner questioning of lost childhood, worldly love, and spiritual aspiration. All my despairing thoughts melted away as I read the book and rode the train through the mountains and valleys of Austria and Switzerland.

Continuing to follow my inner guidance, I ended up in the town of Zermatt, Switzerland. I put my book and my backpack in a locker at the station and wandered into town. My mind was telling me I should find a place to stay before I did anything else, but I felt a force drawing me to the mountains on the other side of town. As I walked through the streets of Zermatt, my life and Hesse's book seemed to merge…

> Alone, Goldmund walked into town. He walked through the unguarded gates, and at the echo of his steps many towns and gates rose up in his memory. He remembered how he had walked through them, how he had

> been received by screaming children, playing boys, quarreling women, the hammering of a forge, the crystal sound of the anvil, the rattling of carts and many other sounds, delicate and coarse, all braided together as though into a web that bore witness to many forms of human labor, joy, bustle, and communication. (Hesse, 1968, p. 203)

Like the characters in the novel, I found myself walking through the town of worldly things, observing life around me while my memories of worldly joys and pain mingled with the sights and sounds around me. Finally, I found myself standing at edge of town looking up at the majestic Matterhorn. I felt like I was standing on the border between the physical world and the spiritual world, between town and mountain, and matter and spirit. My inner and outer journey merged with the story and I realized that my personal struggle was parallel to the classic Christian struggle between flesh and spirit.

> But I say, walk by the Spirit, and do not gratify the desires of the flesh. For the desires of the flesh are against the Spirit, and the desires of the Spirit are against the flesh; for these are opposed to each other, to prevent you from doing what you would. But if you are led by the Spirit you are not under the law. (Galatians 5:16-18)

In that moment, I realized that my thoughts of worldly things tended to block my awareness of guidance. As I looked around me I felt the world of the flesh recede and the world of the spirit emerge. The buildings, the streets, the people, the mountains, all became holy. Without any idea, thought or concern of where I would spend the night, I rode the tram up the mountain in a state of bliss. I got off at the first stop, Black Lake, directly below the mountain peak. The air was fresh, crisp, and thin. Sound seemed to shorten so that mostly a vacuum-like quiet filled the air. I stood at the shore of the lake and gazed under its shimmering mirrored surface. I saw schools of tiny thin fish swimming through waving underwater forests of green flora.

I noticed that two of the fish seemed to be courting each other. They swam side by side, echoing each other's movements. One would move its body in undulating waves, then gently release, and glide. Then the other would follow. Slowly, their dance became synchronized. Their bodies moved in perfect unison, waving and gliding simultaneously. I became lost in their dance, almost feeling as though I were swimming with them. I felt as though the Divine was communicating to me through this experience, giving me a visual expression of the idea of synchronicity and flow. As they fish disappeared from view, I shifted my attention to the panoramic views around me. My mind became empty and the beauty around me filled my awareness.

The next tram arrived, and I felt guided to ride it to the highest peak. A few minutes later I found myself on the top of the world. Below me I could see vast mountain ranges, skiers on sky-high slopes, and misty valleys beneath seas of drifting clouds. I felt as though I was both a part of this vast landscape and that it was all inside of me. I stood there for hours, gazing at the world, meeting fellow travelers, and pondering the beauty of existence. Slowly, storm clouds swept over the valley below and crept up toward the peak I was on. I watched as the clouds enveloped me, surrounding me in soft light and moist air. My skin tingled as though tiny sparks of static electricity were washing over me. I lost the ability to feel where my body ended and the clouds began. I closed my eyes and let myself merge with the clouds, leaving the world of the flesh for a brief moment and becoming one with the world of spirit.

> And after six days Jesus taketh [with him] Peter, and James, and John, and leadeth them up into a high mountain apart by themselves: and he was transfigured before them. (Mark 9:2)

My ecstatic state of consciousness dissipated as I rode the tram down to the town below. A sense of joy and wonder stayed with me and I felt deeply connected to my inner guidance. I walked back into town and was guided to a wonderful pension that had a great room and a reasonable price. I spent the next week following guidance, wondering through the town and mountains, and meeting wonderful people.

After a while, I felt it was time to leave Zermatt. I sat on the train, reading the ending of *Narcissus and Goldmund*,[55] enthralled by Goldmund's journey toward death. A woman with a young boy sat down across from me. I looked up and was stunned by the boy's face. It was burned beyond recognition. Despite the boy's appearance, he was overflowing with exuberance and friendliness. I tried not to stare at his face as he told a fellow traveler about how he was in a bombing in Lebanon. As I finished the last words of Hesse's book and gazed into that child's disfigured face, I found myself awash in thoughts of death and impermanence, falling off the mountain of spirit into the depths of the world of the flesh.

> And now the sick man opened his eyes again and looked for a long while into his friend's face. He said farewell with his eyes. And with a sudden movement, as though he were trying to shake his head, he whispered: 'But how will you die when your time comes…? (Hesse, 1968, p. 311)

The next day I found myself on the shores of the French Riviera, surrounded by the beauty of its scenery and people. It all seemed empty as I sat in a hotel restaurant on the beach of San Rafael lost in despairing thoughts of impermanence, loss, and regret. A middle-aged woman from Oregon asked if she could join me. She asked if I was sad. We talked for hours about God, romantic love, death, and illusion. Her words and presence were very calming and reassuring. As she was leaving, she recommended I take a look at a book called *A Course in Miracles*.[56] I wrote down the information, said goodbye, and went on with my journey.

Months later, back home in Los Angeles, I noticed a large blue book on a friend's coffee table. Its title echoed in my mind, and I remembered it as the book that the woman in San Rafael had recommended. Somehow, I took note of it, and then forgot about it. Several months after this chance event, I was walking through a bookstore after one of my yoga classes, and saw the book again. This time I felt instantly drawn to open it. I slowly picked it up, and opened to the words of the introduction:

> This is a course in miracles. It is a required course. Only the time you take it is voluntary. Free will does not mean that you can establish the curriculum. It means only that you can elect what you want to take at a given time. The course does not aim at teaching the meaning of love, for that is beyond what can be taught. It does aim, however, at removing the blocks to the awareness of love's presence, which is your natural inheritance. The opposite of love is fear, but what is all encompassing can have no opposite. This course can be summed up very simply in this

way: Nothing real can be threatened. Nothing unreal exists. Herein lies the peace of God. (*Course in Miracles*, 1996, Text, p. 1)

These words seemed to penetrate my being. I felt as though the words were written directly to me. The last three sentences resonated in my mind as I recalled a similar phrase from the Hindu scriptures: "The unreal hath no being; the real never ceaseth to be; the truth about both hath been perceived by the seers of the Essence of things."[57] The references to removing the obstacles to love reminded me of my meeting with Baba Hari Dass, only a few weeks earlier. It seemed as though the path of devotion and love that my Kundalini experience was calling me to follow was suddenly in my hands. At once, these two paths merged, and I began a parallel journey of purification, each path feeding the other.

I purchased the book, took it home, opened it, and could not put it down. I read it day and night, driven by some unseen force. Slowly I began to realize that this material was written as though Jesus Christ was the author. I learned that it was channeled material, "… a process in which a person transmits information or artistic expression that he or she receives mentally or physically and which appears to come from a personality source outside the conscious mind."[58] The communication process of channeling has been a component of many experiences of prophecy and divination throughout history.

As I continued to read through the text I was split between my skeptical mind and a growing sense that this book was written by something other than a human being. Deciding to just go with my feelings, I began the daily lessons in the workbook portion of the book. Slowly, I started to notice that my everyday experiences were resonating with the daily lessons, as though an unseen instructor was creating experiential teaching examples. "Every situation, properly perceived, becomes an opportunity to heal the Son of God."[59]

While the Course is written in Christian terminology, it redefines these terms and holds itself as a psycho-spiritual training and not a religion. I found myself drawn to this training with a devotion I had not known before. I could not start my day without my daily lesson. My perception of things started to shift, and I became more and more aware of divine guidance entering my daily life. This guidance became a direct process as the lessons went on, incorporating meditative and prayer methods of invoking guidance. This process of accessing divine guidance culminates with the final lesson:

> This holy instant would I give to You. Be You in charge. For I would follow You, Certain that Your direction gives me peace. And if I need a word to help me, He will give it to me. If I need a thought, that will He also give. And if I need but stillness and a tranquil open mind, these are the gifts I will receive of Him. He is in charge by my request. And He will hear and answer me, because He speaks for God my Father and His holy Son. (*Course in Miracles*, 1996, Workbook, p. 486)

When I finished this final lesson I took a walk along the Venice Beach boardwalk and watched the sunset. I felt peaceful and inspired. As the sun sank into the Pacific Ocean and the sky turned bright crimson, I kept repeating the final lesson in my mind. On my way home, I stopped by a side street as my attention was drawn to a lone human figure curled up on the ground of a neon lit parking lot across the way. It was a cold night, and the body shivered in the waning light.

Moving closer, I could see that the lone figure was a homeless woman, huddled on the ground and struggling to stay warm. Suddenly, a clear inner voice said: "You have an extra blanket in your car." Without hesitation I walked to my car, got the blanket, walked back to the parking lot, and slowly approached the homeless woman. Her eyes were closed and she was mumbling to herself. I gently covered her with the blanket and silently prayed for her. She opened her eyes and looked at me as though I were an angel who had just answered her prayers. I felt a wave of gratitude flow from her and envelop my heart. I smiled and gestured as if to say "you're welcome." Tears streamed down her face as she wrapped herself in the blanket and closed her eyes to sleep.

I walked away and down the boardwalk, feeling as though I were a transparent being floating on air. People stared at me strangely as I passed. Many of them turned around to look at me as if they sensed my presence from behind. For the next few days, I felt an indescribable sense of peace. This experience gave me a powerful lesson in one of the Course's basic tenants: "To give and to receive are one in truth."[60] I had given away an old blanket and received an inner warmth beyond compare.

> The Holy Spirit has the power to change the whole foundation of the world you see to something else; a basis not insane, on which a sane perception can be based, another world perceived. And one in which nothing is contradicted that would lead the Son of God to sanity and joy. Nothing attests to death and cruelty; to separation and to difference. For here is everything perceived as one, and no one loses that each one may gain. (*Course in Miracles*, 1996, Text, p. 532)

Over the next several years, I continued my work with the Course, repeatedly practicing the daily lessons, and reading the "Text" and the "Manual for Teachers" sections of the material. I continually had the sense of undergoing a process of *transcendent education*, in which an *inner teacher* was guiding me to "… break the stubborn habits of a lifetime."[61] This process seemed to go far beyond just the use of everyday experiences as a teaching tool. It was as though a grand curriculum was guiding my whole life. Various mystics and saints from many different traditions have reported similar transcendent educational experiences.[62]

My work with the Course seemed to be centered on the striping away of my fearful perceptions of the world, which were blocking my experience of love. I experienced this process through the healing of my relationships with others. The guidance I received during this transcendent educational training came in the form of an inner voice, visions, synchronistic events, and by asking for guidance and then opening the Course book at random, a process of divination called bibliomancy.[63]

Shortly after my experience with the homeless woman on the beach, I traveled to Toronto to visit with a young woman I had been seeing romantically on and off for several years. I had met her days after returning from my first trip to Esalen and fell swiftly into an addictive pattern with her. When I was with her I felt joy beyond compare but when we were apart I felt empty, lost, and paranoid. She was a child of alcoholic parents who was caught in her own pattern of emotional reaching out and withdrawal. I had ridden the emotional roller coaster with her for several years, and not even my journey to Europe had shaken the love madness from my heart.

Finally, I was traveling to visit her home and family. On the airplane I prayed for a way to heal my relationship with her. I closed my eyes and opened the Course book at random and was deeply touched by the words on the page. "When you feel the holiness of your relationship is threatened by anything, stop instantly and offer the Holy Spirit your willingness, in spite of fear, to let Him exchange this instant for the holy one that you would rather have."[64] As I continued to read, the Text described a process of guidance to be used when troubles arose in a relationship.

> Whoever is saner at the time the threat is perceived should remember how deep is his indebtedness to the other and how much gratitude is due him, and be glad that he can pay his debt by bringing happiness to both. Let him remember this and say: I desire this holy instant for myself that I may share it with my brother, whom I love. It is not possible that I can have it without him, or he without me.
> Yet it is wholly possible for us to share it now. And so I choose this instant as the one to offer the Holy Spirit that His blessing may descend on us, and keep us both in peace. (*Course in Miracles*, 1996, Text, p. 384)

When I arrived in Toronto, I used this guidance process constantly. Each time I used it, the distance between us would miraculously disappear. She would stop withdrawing and my clinging urges melted away. By the time my visit was over I felt much closer to her while feeling more accepting of any distances that would arise between us. From Toronto I flew to Chicago to visit with my family, where the young woman and I finally ended the relationship over the phone. Through my work with the Course I was able to express my hurt and anger and begin the healing process.

In Chicago, I stayed with my parents in my childhood home again. My mother had been diagnosed with an unknown degenerative brain disease and was starting to slip away. As I sat with her and tried to tell her everything I needed to tell her, an inner voice gently arose within me, telling me to "move back home and spend time with my mother and heal our relationship." I returned to Los Angeles and once more put all my belongings in storage. Driving back home across the country, I had no regrets about leaving the highs and lows of the film business again.

I spent the next several months being with my mother and the rest of my family. My relationship with my mother deepened and I was able to express my love and gratitude. We took walks together and I sat with her for many hours in conversation and in silence. I would often silently practice my daily lessons from the Course while being in my mother's presence and wordlessly send her prayers of love. I frequently sensed a presence within me and between us that felt like Jesus. This presence would guide me with an inner voice, reminding me to see past my mother's condition and see the light in her. Miraculously when I held this consciousness she seemed to be more present and "normal."

One day, the family was all together having dinner, someone made a joke about Jesus and my mom blurted out "Mark is Jesus!" There was a long moment of awkward silence as my family tried to figure out if she was making a joke or if this was another manifestation of her illness. My mom looked at me and smiled. I could feel her silently saying to me "I know…" The awkward silence gradually gave way to casual conversation while my mom and I shared a sacred moment across the table.

As I healed my relationship with my mother, I also worked with the Course on forgiveness and release for my recently dissolved romantic relationship with the young woman from Toronto. Slowly I reached a state in which I no longer looked at women as merely objects of desire or potential mates. I began to see them as simply other human beings. Months later, while spending the winter with my parents at our home in Florida, I met my future wife, Sarah.

We met on an elevator in the building where both our parents had apartments. Sarah, her mother, and I were heading up to our respective floors. Sarah and I exchanged hellos and then went on our way. I remember thinking how good it felt to look at a beautiful woman as just another person. Later that evening, her mother called and asked if I would ask her daughter out.

Sarah apologized for her mothers' forwardness and gave me an opportunity to decline. I felt it would be nice to hang out with someone my own age and asked her to a jazz club the following night. Over the next few weeks we hung out together and became great friends. During this time I constantly worked with the daily lessons, writing them on index cards and stealing glances at them throughout the day. One day Sarah asked me what was on the index cards I kept taking out of my pocket and reading. I told her about the Course and we had many thoughtful conversions about God, love, and life.

One night, while having a drink in a bar on the beach, we were sitting at a booth engrossed in one of our conversations. Suddenly I found myself kissing her. It was as though one moment we were talking and the next we were in the middle of a kiss. I felt like some great magnetic force had instantly pulled us together. We kissed for a long time, then slowly released. We both let out a sigh and Sarah slid off her seat and under the table. We laughed and from that moment on, we were a couple. After a while, I asked Sarah to come back to Los Angeles with me. She said yes and we jumped in my Volkswagen van and headed west.

The first night on the road we stopped at a hotel for the night. While Sarah freshened up in the bathroom I meditated on that day's lesson in the Course: "I am not a body. I am free."[65] As I read about using the body as a means of communication, I entered a deep altered state. Sarah came into the room. As we kissed I repeated the lesson in my mind and I felt our two bodies melt together. That night we made love for the first time and I felt as though I had never truly made love before that moment.

The next couple weeks on the road were filled with miracles. Sarah began to study the Course with me and we meditated together every day. At the end of each meditation we both would hear the sound of the ocean in our heads. We felt connected with each other and guided at every turn, meeting incredible people and seeing wondrous sights. The experience was very similar to my flow experiences in Europe but this time it was a shared experience. I felt a love that was deep and gentle, passionate and serene.

A year later we were married and heading back to Florida for our honeymoon trip. My relationships with the women in my life had deepened and old wounds were slowly healing. As Sarah and I drove back down the road we had traveled before, I began to feel anxious about my relationship with my father. I had always felt a great distance between us and my inner voice was telling me that it was time to deal with my relationship with both my inner and outer father.

I kept asking for guidance on how to heal the relationship. I prayed and listened for the inner voice but nothing was coming. Even the random opening of the Course book seemed to be failing me. Finally, mentally exhausted, I asked Sarah to take over driving. I put on an audiotape from the Course by Marianne Williamson[66] and laid back in the passenger seat and closed my eyes, feeling a deep sense of surrender.

> We see in the middle of our mind a little ball of golden light. We watch this light as it begins to grow, larger and larger, until it now covers the inner vision of our mind. We see for ourselves, within this light, a beautiful temple. We see a garden that surrounds the temple and a body of water that flows through the garden. We see that the inside of the temple is lit by this same beautiful golden light. And here we are, drawn together by the power and in the presence of God. (Williamson, 1987)

As I listened to the familiar words of the opening meditation of the tape, I began to enter a deep altered state. The usual images that arose during the meditation suddenly turned into a clear and powerful vision that was unlike any of my previous experiences. I was floating above a beautiful landscape. Directly beneath me I saw a building shaped like the six-pointed Jewish Star of David with a glass dome on top patterned after the Taoist Yin-Yang symbol. Two three-story triangles were built one on top of the other to form the Star of David from above. The Yin/Yang glass dome on the roof housed a beautiful Temple with gardens, a stream running through it, and a ball of golden light imbedded in the center of the dome.

Surrounding the building was a crystal blue reflecting pool. Its water gently flowed under the wood and glass deck encircling the building into a circular rock cavern below. Suspended in this cavern of rock, waterfalls, and gardens were the six lower floors of the building. Within the structure I envisioned a library, cafe, dramatic theater, movie house, art gallery, storytelling garden, poetry reading room, meditation rooms, massage rooms, yoga/martial arts studio, an altered states mind gym, a chapel, community rooms, and a temple.

I opened my eyes and began to attempt to draw the structure I envisioned. The next few days on the road I continued to have visions of this structure and spent hours committing the images and ideas to paper. As the vision flowed through me a name for the work also arose within me, I was to call it the *Ark of Consciousness*.[67] When we arrived in Florida I showed my drawings to my father since he had been an engineer, architect, and general contractor all his life. He became excited about the idea and spent hours with me discussing it. As we sat on the patio, huddled together over the drawings, I felt an incredible sense of connection with him.

Through the years I had struggled to connect with my father, frustrated by our inability to deeply share our thoughts and feelings with each other. Now, suddenly, I felt as if we had reached that depth, but in a different, unspoken way. This experience and several readings from the Course brought the realization that I had been trying to heal my relationship with my father in the same way I had done with my mother. To heal my relationship with my mother I had needed to fully express my thoughts and feelings. Slowly it became clear to me that what was necessary for the healing of the relationship with my father was a surrender of my expectations of who I thought he should be and an acceptance of who he was.

> And he is healed because you offered faith to him, giving him to the Holy Spirit and releasing him from every demand your ego would make of him. Thus do you see him free, and in this vision does the Holy Spirit share. And since He shares it He has given it, and so He heals through you. (*Course in Miracles*, 1996, Text, p. 398)

While seeking the holiness within my self and others through my work with the Course, I also sojourned through the world of traditional and modern Christianity by attending Church services from several denominations with my Christian friends and delving into both classical and modern Christian Literature. I read the New Testament and the works of Brother Lawrence, Thomas Merton, Brother David Steindl-Rast,[68] and many others and found profound inspiration and deep lessons on guidance.

> Ask, and it will be given you;
> seek, and you will find;
> knock, and the door will be opened to you.
> For everyone who asks, receives;
> and he who seeks, finds;

> and to him who knocks,
> the door will be opened.
> - Matthew 7:7-8[69]

Little did I know that all my seeking and knocking on spirit's door would lead me into a long dark night of the soul that began in the summer of 1990. My mother's health had been gradually deteriorating for years, and my father, having taken care of her through it all, finally reached his breaking point. My family decided it was time to put my mother in a nursing home. I flew home to see if I could help. The situation had reached a point of crisis and nothing I said or did seemed to make a difference. I meditated as often as I could and prayed for guidance without ceasing, yet all my effort seemed in vain...my connection was lost. The people at the nursing home advised us not to tell my mother we were taking her to the home until we showed up at the door. In my heart I knew this was wrong, but all my efforts to find another way failed.

The moment we approached the home, my mother began to scream and cry. I had never seen her so terrified. I had never seen any human being so terrified. She grabbed my arm and clung to me like a frightened child, begging me to keep her out of the home. Even though I convinced my family to stop for a moment, and go out to eat and discuss the situation, it seemed that the nursing home was an inevitable outcome. As we finally brought my mother into the home, her broken spirit penetrated my whole being. Something deep inside me shattered, and the person I thought I was, was gone forever. This experience was the start of a powerful spiritual crisis.

> How is it that emotional crises lead to spiritual [emergence] experiences? Intense emotional experiences open us to the profound mystery of life itself...the visible order that had defined our world is suddenly gone. It is as if the ship–our personal identity–has burned, and we are

suddenly submerged in the powerful ocean of our raw emotions and unconscious forces. (Bragdon, 1990, p.120)

When I returned to Los Angeles, everything seemed different…both inside and without. Worldly pursuits felt empty and meaningless to me. The everyday activities of life became an overwhelming burden. Even my spiritual practices that had guided and supported me in the past seemed to have lost all their power. I experienced waves of intense emotions and visions of other worlds. One day I was walking down a busy street, feeling lost and internally crying for help. I felt drawn to a bookstore window. As I approached the window and looked at the sea of books, my eyes were guided to one particular book that appeared to stand out amongst the rest.

The title of the book, *The stormy search for the self : A guide to personal growth through transformational crisis*,[70] sent a chill down my spine, and my heart filled with gratitude as I experienced a moment of long sought after guidance. The book helped me understand that I was going through a spiritual emergency, a series of "critical and experientially difficult stages of a profound psychological transformation that involves one's entire being."[71] I learned that I had gone through many emergence episodes in the past as I read about the different forms spiritual emergencies take.

The authors of the book, Stanislav and Christina Grof, list ten distinct types of spiritual emergency: Shamanic crisis; Kundalini awakening; episodes of unitive consciousness (mystical/peak experiences); psychological renewal; psychic opening; communication with spirit or spirits; near-death experiences; UFO encounter experiences; and possession states.[72] The intensities of these experiences seem to vary; sometimes they are strong experiential episodes along a gradual path of emergence, and other times they appear as powerful, crisis producing encounters.

All the experiences that I was presently going through were there before me in black and white, and suddenly I didn't feel alone or insane. Knowing that I was going through an evolutionary crisis along the spiritual path[73] helped me reframe my experience in a positive light, and enabled me to more consciously work with it. Using the book's resources, I was able to find a transpersonal therapist who assisted me in my spiritual emergence process, and helped me recognize and begin to answer the "call" of this profound crisis of transformation to grow "…toward higher levels of functioning and perceiving life."[74]

I decided to go on retreat for a while and find a way to listen the inner call of the emergence process that was coursing through my entire being. I drove up the coast and was drawn to Esalen Institute once again. By nightfall, I was soaking in the hot baths on the cliffs above the ocean. Waves of sadness and peace and meaning and meaninglessness swept through me, as the hot mineral water melted some of the emotional stress and trauma that had been residing in my muscles. I looked up at the vast canopy of stars above me and tears came to my eyes as I prayed for help.

The next morning I woke up at dawn and soaked in the baths again. After breakfast I walked around the grounds in a state of gentle sorrow. I meditated for a while and then walked around some more, letting my impulses guide me. I ended up in a small grove of eucalyptus trees. I stopped for a moment and breathed in the sweet smell of the trees. I looked up and saw hundreds of monarch butterflies swarming in the trees above my head. All my stress and anxieties melted away as I entered a state of awe and wonder. Tears came to my eyes as the beauty of the moment and the fluttering lightness of the butterflies filled me.

After an hour or so I continued my wondering, through patches of sun and grass into the waterfall canyon and down to the ocean. For the next few days I fluttered around Esalen, meditating, soaking in the baths, walking in nature, and having deep conversations with fellow seekers. I felt nurtured by it all, but I also felt sad. It felt as though I had left the path for a long time and was returning wounded; and even though the path was familiar, I felt like a stranger.

One morning I was sitting alone having breakfast, feeling lost and wondering what to do and where to go next, when I overheard people talking about going to a Gregorian chanting session with Brother David Steindl-Rast. The next thing I knew I was sitting in a circle being bathed with the deep reverberating sounds of Gregorian chant. Brother David's gentle spirit and the penetrating soul of the chanting touched me deeply. The chanting seemed to open up a stream of old emotions within me and for the next few days my ups and downs seemed more extreme. My prayers became deeper emotionally, as I called on God and Jesus to help me with tears in my heart. For the next few days, memories of past inabilities to love and to be loved washed over me, and I could feel my heart struggling to open with each passing moment, with each human encounter, and with each natural wonder small and great.

A week later, after some wandering up and down the coast, I found my way to Brother David's monastery, New Camaldoli Immaculate Heart Hermitage, located on a hilltop above the ocean several miles south of Esalen. I checked in as a retreatant and attended the Vespers service. I felt very uncomfortable during the service, which seemed to be filled with the ideas of sacrifice, sin and punishment. The monks seemed so inward and I felt a cold distance between us. I repeated the days lesson from the Course in Miracles, "I offer only miracles today, for I would have them be returned to me," as I prayed for them and for me. As I saw them in the light of love and forgiveness, their beautiful and haunting voices blessed me with peace.

The next morning I woke up feeling more rested than I had in a long time. The sky was bright and clear above the monastery while a thick blanket of clouds covered the ocean below. The birds were singing as I watched a hawk gently glide above the hills and sweep out in wide circles across the cloud covered ocean. The clouds seemed so soft and fluffy, like God had placed a warm cotton quilt upon the sea to keep it safe. The day's lesson resonated in my mind, "Today the peace of God envelops me, and I forget all things except His Love."

I attended the Eucharist Service. It was beautiful. We stood in a circle around the altar while one of the monks spoke of the blood and body of Christ. All the monks seemed to be in an altered state as they went around the circle hugging each other and the guests. As each one hugged me and whispered "Peace be with you" I went deeper and deeper into a state of profound inner peace. Then we all lined up and received the blood and body of Christ. As I drank the wine and ate the bread I experienced what felt like a metaphysical transformation of matter into spirit, as though the energy of the Christ entered me and became me and I became it. After the service I walked around the grounds in a state of grace; my mind was empty and I was filled with a sense of peace. I went to the library and opened up a book by Thomas Merton and began to read:

> Contemplation is ... the response to a call: a call from Him Who has no voice, and yet Who speaks in everything that is, and Who, most of all, speaks in the depths of our own being: for we ourselves are words of His. (Merton, 1961, p.3)

In the evening I went to Vespers again but this time it was wonderful, filled with words of peace and rebirth. As the talk centered on Jesus and Jerusalem I had a powerful vision. I was walking through the streets of Jerusalem dressed as Jesus. Rockets streaked through the sky and bombs fell all around me. At first everyone was frightened, but when they saw me they became calm. Some were angry, but when they approached me, peace swept through them. Then the bombing stopped and I walked to the temple with a crowd following me. I spoke to the multitudes and asked that Jerusalem become a city of the world, not a part of any country, nor the property of any one faith or people, a neutral land owned by all the people of the Earth, free and open to all humanity. The vision faded and my awareness returned to the service. I had a powerful felt sense that the presence of the Divine was within me and that this presence was the answer to my prayers for help, assuring me that I did not walk alone.

I spent the rest of the week in deep contemplation; walking around the grounds, going to services, meditating, studying the works of Thomas Merton and Brother Laurence, and practicing being in the presence of the Divine. The stress and anxiety left me, and for a brief time my emotional storm vanished and I felt the Divine speaking to me from deep within me and through every exterior experience and encounter. For a time it was just me and the Divine; every person, every rock and every tree was the Divine speaking to me.

> Now he lives as if there were no one but God and he in the world, he converses everywhere with God, asks Him for what he needs, and rejoices with Him ceaselessly in a thousand ways … this conversation with God occurs in the depth and center of the soul. It is there that the soul speaks to God heart to heart, and
> always in a great and profound peace that the soul enjoys in God. (Brother Lawrence of the Resurrection, 1978, p. 89)

When I returned to Los Angeles I had a renewed sense of purpose and felt drawn to change the course of my life by concentrating more fully on service and healing, both for myself and for others. During this time, I learned more about my emergence experiences and began to explore opportunities to study transpersonal psychology. I applied to the Institute of Transpersonal Psychology in Palo Alto and was accepted into their program. Then I experienced another stage of my spiritual crisis.

    Gradually I began to realize that my inner urgings to focus on personal growth and transformational learning were in direct conflict with the outer world around me. If I were to choose the path of my inner urgings I would have to do so without a penny in my pocket, and against the advice and support of my family and friends. I was also up against an internal battle between my own perceptions and feelings of security, faith, success, and failure. In the end, I chose to make the "logical" choice and postpone school for a year in order to earn enough money to pay for it. I took a job editing a feature film in New York, and unknowingly began the next and most powerful stage of my spiritual crisis.

> Into this dark night, souls begin to enter
> when God draws them forth from the state of beginners
> …and begins to set them in the state of progressives…
> to the end that, after passing through it,
> they may arrive at the state of the perfect,
> which is that of the Divine union
> of the soul with God.
> - *St. John of the Cross*[75]

The night before getting on the plane for New York, a moment of terror rippled through my body. All at once, I felt that this was going to be a rough journey, while I also had the sense that it was one I had to take. I arrived in New York armed with two suitcases and a piece of paper with the address of my destination, somewhere in Manhattan. I took a taxi to the address that was supposed to be the production office and editing room. We pulled up to an old tenement house, whose deteriorating structure was semi-hidden under a fresh coat of thick paint. The taxi driver grabbed my money, threw my suitcases on the cracked sidewalk, and drove off. There I was, in the heart of a neighborhood called "Hell's Kitchen," about to work on a film called *Chain of Desire*.[76] I look back on this experience now and smile at the wonderful symbolism.

As I knocked on the burnt red door, I experienced a wave of panic. I inwardly asked for some sign to guide me through this. Just then the landlady opened the door and greeted me. She was very kind, and handed me the keys to the first floor apartment that had been turned into the editing room. As I glanced down at the key chain in my hand, I had to smile. There, at the end of the key chain, was a plastic encased picture of Jesus, his hand held up palm open. I felt an inner voice say: "it will be okay...stay." I experienced a gentle calmness, as I entered the apartment.

When I met the producer he explained that my apartment wasn't ready yet, so they had to put me up in a hotel down the block for the first few weeks. I settled into my hotel, got a good nights' sleep, and began my work the next day. The next eighteen days were an inner and outer battle as I struggled to edit footage of a film exploring the weakness of the human senses, while desperately attempting to stay out of the crossfire of the intense political and artistic conflicts between and within the producers and director. Gradually I experienced a sense of "psychic fatigue" as my consciousness was enveloped in the awareness of impermanence and suffering.

Finally, on the nineteenth day, my apartment was ready and they moved me out of the hotel and into the upstairs front room of the tenement house. As the sun set on Hell's Kitchen, I glanced through the windows of the building across the street, and watched as several lonely people came home after a hard day to their empty apartments or distant relationships. On the sidewalk below my window, a stream of prostitutes, pushers, and homeless people slowly emerged with the encroaching darkness of night. Large black cockroaches roamed the walls, floors, and ceiling of my room. Giant strands of dust wafted through the air as stagnant heat rose out of the rusting radiators. I spent the entire night wide awake, listening to gun shots, sirens, and screams of anger and despair, while experiencing waves of intense sorrow, haunting visions, and deep existential stirrings. I felt myself descending into the darkest shadows of humanity and myself. Yet somehow, amidst this darkest of dark moments, I felt an invisible hand holding me, guiding me through it all.

> In the stress and anguish of the Night, when it turns back from the vision of the Infinite to feel again the limitations of the finite the self loses the power to Do; and learns to surrender its will to the operation of a larger Life, that it may Be. (Underhill, 1961; p.388-389)

In the morning, as I watched the city reawaken from its' madness, I experienced a profound shift within myself. Suddenly, I felt a sorrow as vast as the entire planet and as deep as all human history. I cried at the awareness of the impermanence of everything I could touch, taste, smell, hear, or see. I wept as all the thoughts, perceptions, and ideals I once held to be true washed away into a void of unknowing. I felt a gentle calmness as I entered a deep altered state in which I felt a distance from all physical form, while having a sense of the hidden unity that swims under the surface of things. Without thought or doubt, I packed my bags, quit my job, and flew back to Los Angeles.

Back in my familiar surroundings, I went to doctors to make sure that what was happening to me was not some kind of physical problem. They could not find any organic causes of my condition but recommended I go on anti-depression drugs. Having studied the theories of spiritual emergence and emergency, I knew that this route would not be advantageous for my growth and healing. Instead of the drugs, I began my healing and work-study retreat at Esalen, and received the many wonderful experiences of healing and "fruitful union" that is said to arise following the dark night.[77]

> The self, deprived of "perception, knowledge, will, work, self-seeking"--the I, the Me, the Mine--loses itself, denies itself, unforms itself, drawing "ever nearer" to the One, till "nothing is to be seen but a ground which rests upon itself"--the ground of the soul, in which it has union with God. (Underhill, 1961, p. 400-401)

A close friend of mine offered to drive me up to Esalen to begin my healing retreat. On the way up I felt like I was leaving the world and heading to an unknown realm. I had lost all sense of the person I thought I was. When we drove down the inclined road into Esalen I felt as though I was entering a sacred space; I could feel a subtle field of energy mixing with the crisp ocean air and the lush woods that created a holy atmosphere that seemed to surround me and hold me. I felt safe for the first time in years and my whole body relaxed.

At the end of the first week I spoke to my father over the phone and he asked if he could come visit me. I agreed and he made the arrangements to stay at Esalen for the following weekend. After hanging up the phone I felt sick to my stomach and I was gripped with fear about my father's visit. While I had made great strides in releasing my expectations of him, I still had a great deal of unconscious issues with him that played on my being like a strong ocean undercurrent. I prayed for help and guidance using various *Course in Miracles* practices, and tried to surrender my inner process and my attachments to outcome. By the time my father arrived I had reached a state of relative inner calm.

My father and I spent the whole weekend together. At first we had the normal superficial interactions that were characteristic of our relationship. As we interacted I silently repeated a few select passages from the Course inviting the Holy Spirit into our relationship. Then one afternoon, while walking around the grounds, I felt a Holy presence fill the space between my father and myself, my mind emptied of all thought, and I was able to just be with my father as a human being. I grew comfortable with the silence between us and let go of trying to fill the empty space.

Suddenly my father started to talk about the struggles around my mother's worsening health condition. As he told me that my sisters were begging him to take my mother off life support, he began to cry. He said he just couldn't do it. He couldn't take her life. I shared with him my feelings about the situation and that I didn't know if I could do it either. As we sat together in silence, surrounded by wind swept trees and the sound of the ocean below, the sorrow I felt about the situation mixed with a deep sense of awe and gratefulness for finally connecting with my father on such a deep level.

For the rest of my father's visit we shifted between deep personal talks, superficial conversation, and silence. I was accepting of all the different states of our relationship and felt a profound sense of peace and connection with him. All the years of blame I had placed on my father for not being the sort of person I wished he were seemed to melt away. While these experiences of intimacy were brief interludes amidst my ongoing struggle to heal my relationship with my father, they have become seeds of healing that are gently blossoming within and between my father and myself.

> Think but how holy you must be from whom the Voice for God calls lovingly unto your brother, that you may awake in him the Voice that answers to your call! And think how holy he must be when in him sleeps your own

> salvation, with his freedom joined! However much you wish he be condemned, God is in him. And never will you know He is in you as well while you attack His chosen home, and battle with His host. Regard him gently. Look with loving eyes on him who carries Christ within him, that you may behold his glory and rejoice that Heaven is not separate from you. (*Course in Miracles*, 1996, Text, p. 560)

The next several months at Esalen were amazing and I experienced a profound healing of my spiritual crisis: I had numerous transformative experiences, including the shamanic and yogic processes I previously discussed; I met wonderful people who gave me love, encouragement and support; The workshops and seminars gently shifted my perception of myself and the world; and the sacred natural environment filled me with its energetic healing salve.

During the last week of my stay I was moved to a bunkroom for retreat guests since my work-study program had ended. One of my new roommates was a devout born-again Christian. We had several talks about Jesus and the Christian way. One afternoon, as I returned to our cabin, I heard yelling coming from inside the cabin. I hesitated and asked for guidance. I felt a strong pull to go inside while I also felt a sense of danger. I opened the door to find my Christian friend screaming at our other roommates, telling them that they would go to hell if they do not accept Jesus into their lives. I tried to calm him down, but instead he focused his rage on me. He started to speak as if he were Jesus, condemning our roommates, the whole world, and me.

The other roommates slowly sneaked out of the cabin and I started to back up toward the door. All I could do was try to calm him down and pray within for help. Somehow I was able to hold him with compassion as he railed against me. Without realizing it, I had managed to leave the cabin. The young man did not follow me out, though he continued to yell. His voice echoed around the property and people started to look our way. I prayed for a way to help him. I walked down the path and suddenly saw Brother David Steindl-Rast a few steps away. I told Brother David about the situation and lead him to the cabin. The young man was standing outside, pacing back and forth while talking to himself.

Brother David gently approached the young man and started to speak to him in a soft and reassuring voice. I watched with amazement as he calmed him down. It seemed as though Brother David's presence ushered in a container of peace that enveloped all of us. The young man explained that God had told him he was Jesus and that those who didn't believe in him would suffer eternal damnation. I can't remember Brother David's reply to the young man. I only remember that his words seemed to come from a deep and profound Source, and that I had the sense that I was witnessing a living example of the discernment between the Voice of the Divine and the voice of illusion.

> Do not be conformed to this world,
> but be transformed by the renewing of your minds,
> so that you may discern what is the Will of God.
> *- Romans 12:2*

Discernment is a major issue in the process of divine guidance, and I soon discovered that the Christian tradition has a very extensive science of discernment developed from the scriptures and the writings of Saints.[78] One of the most notable works in this science is *The Spiritual Exercises of Saint Ignatius*.[79] Saint Ignatius explored the process of "... preparing and disposing the soul to free itself of all inordinate attachments, and after accomplishing this, of seeking and discovering the Divine Will..."[80] Within this process he developed guidelines and rules for the discerning of the spirits, which have become the foundation for Christian discernment.⁸¹ These guidelines and rules of discernment cover both the process of seeking guidance and that of discerning the authenticity of such guidance. One of these guidelines for authenticity holds that true guidance is rooted in love.⁸² I saw so clearly that Brother David was speaking and moving out of a deep sense of love, while the young man appeared to be lost in a dark well of fear and anger.

> The Word, received in faith, falls as seed into the silent soil of hope and brings fruit in love. There is no willfulness in love's action only a willingness to bear fruit. (Steindl-Rast, 1984, p. 177)

As I watched Brother David bring the light of love to this young man's darkness, I felt my own spiritual darkness dissolve. A sense of wonder washed over me and I understood that the Divine had been with me every step of the way, and that even the darkness was sacred. I realized that this young man's darkness was a gift toward my awakening, and I learned that guidance could come in the form of a lack of guidance or a withdrawing of divine conciliation, which then acts as a catalyst for deeper growth and transformation.⁸³ I also learned that guidance can come in the form of profound emotional life experiences, which have the ability to call us to awaken to a higher level of being.⁸⁴

Many Paths, One Road

My experiences at Esalen during this extended healing and work-study retreat seemed to bring me to a threshold of transformation. I had the sense that I was crossing a kind of bridge ... completing several processes while beginning several more. Before the retreat I had the sense that I was searching for something far beyond my reach. During the retreat I felt as though that something was suddenly within my grasp. The short glimpses of the spiritual realm now unfolded into an ongoing stream within and around me that was just waiting for my attention.

The several traditions I had been previously exploring appeared to reach a climax during this time, while many more traditions entered my field of consciousness. The road from this point forward became a single road of many paths. I began to study and explore many of the world's spiritual traditions, incorporating them into an eclectic practice while continuing my core guidance practice from the Course in Miracles. Each new spiritual tradition I encountered seemed to offer me a different view of the Divine that gradually coalesced into a more expansive view of the sacred. Additionally, it seemed as though each tradition was entering my life to give me a specific experiential lesson about the Divine and my relation with it.

> Experience is a riverbed,
> Its source hidden,
> forever flowing:
> Its entrance,
> the root of the world,
> The Way moves within it:
> Draw upon it;
> it will not run dry.
> - *Lao Tzu*[85]

The Way of the Tao

My first exposure to Taoism occurred during the first week of my healing retreat at Esalen. I signed up for a workshop in human potential with John Heider, author of *The Tao of Leadership*.[86] I had no idea what the experience would be like, but somehow I was drawn to it. During the first session I found myself profoundly moved by the process. At first I couldn't put my finger on what it was that was touching me so deeply.

Slowly I realized that there was an atmosphere within the group that seemed to have a life of its own, moving us in ways beyond our comprehension. Later, John introduced us to this atmosphere, which he called the group field, and explained how this field is the divine flow that the Taoist's call the Tao, or the way of things. I picked up a copy of his book at the bookstore and began to study the written text and the way John employed it in practice.

> Learn to see emptiness. When you enter an empty house, can you feel the mood of the place? It is the same with a vase or a pot; learn to see the emptiness inside, which is the usefulness of it. People's speech and actions are figural events. They give the group form and content. The silences and empty spaces, on the other hand, reveal the group's essential mood, the context for everything that happens. That is the group field. (Heider, 1985, p.21)

I began to slowly gain a sense of this field within the group and surrender to it. The experience was very similar to the divine flow experiences I had previously encountered, but now it was with a whole group of people. My ability to sense the field also extended beyond the group into the rest of my life. I gained an awareness of a subtle energy that flowed within me and around me. When I finished the workshop and John's book, I delved into the *Tao Te Ching*, one of Taoism's essential texts.[87] Eventually, I extended my Taoist study into the areas of the Chinese energy awareness practices of *Tai Chi Chuan* and *Chi Qong*.[88]

Through my study of the Tao Te Ching, continued energy awareness practices, and additional group field processes, I gained access to a new channel of divine guidance and more conscious ability to enter a divine flow state. I began to realize that this divine flow state was the guidance itself. I suddenly understood that being in the flow, or surrendering to the way of things, was a process of continual and simultaneous seeking, receiving, and following of divine guidance. When I would shift into this awareness by entering a state of emptiness, I would feel a certainty of purpose and safety no matter how uncertain or threatening things appeared. I had a sense of moving past communicating with the Divine, and into a state of being in which the Divine was like a vast moving stream within and around me.

> The Tao gives birth to all beings,
> nourishes them, maintains them,
> cares for them, comforts them, protects them,
> takes them back to itself,
> creating without possessing,
> acting without expecting,
> guiding without interfering.
> That is why love of the Tao
> is in the very nature of things.
> - Lao Tzu[89]

The Sufi Path

While I was expanding my understanding of and ability to surrender to this way of being, the wisdom of the Sufi path entered my life and added another dimension to my awareness of this process. About halfway through my Esalen healing retreat I entered a state of struggle. I suddenly lost my ability to empty myself and connect with the divine flow. About this time a friend of mine gave me the gift of a Sufi poem. I had never heard of Sufism before and didn't know what to expect. As I read the poem my consciousness began to shift. Somehow this poem felt like a message from the Divine, giving me a clue to what my obstacle was: Once again, I was struggling to empty; I was reaching up to touch the Divine; and I was desperately seeking the connection ... when all I had to do was let go.

> The clear bead at the center changes everything.
> There are no edges to my loving now.
> I've heard it said there's a window that opens
> from one mind to another,
> but if there's no wall,
> there's no need for fitting the window, or the latch.
> - Jalal al-Din Rumi, 511 (1984)

I was learning a great paradox on the path: While one must seek in order to find, in order to find, one must give up seeking.[90] Indeed, this idea began to shed a great deal of light on my past experiences in which I achieved a state of divine connection only after reaching a point of total surrender of the search itself.

> O seeker, know that the path to Truth is within you. You are the traveler. Going happens by itself. Coming happens to you, without you.
> There is no arriving or leaving; nor is there any place; nor is there a contained within a container. Who is there to be with God? What is there other than God? Who seeks and finds when there is none but God? - Sheikh Badruddin (Fadiman & Frager, 1997, p.198)

The Sufi path communicated this wisdom to me through its teachings, poems, and sacred stories. The words would penetrate my whole being, teaching me about the qualities of emptiness and surrender. Certain phrases, poems, and stories would become part of my consciousness, rising into my awareness in the midst of experiences. In this way, they became oracles of divine guidance. I would be in the middle of a situation, wondering what direction I should go, when all of a sudden a Sufi message would arise in my consciousness, and give me a broader perspective within which I could easily see the way to proceed.

One such story is the *Tale of the Sands*.[91] I first encountered this powerful teaching story in a class on Sufism. As we read through it, I felt as though I was being immersed in a stream of higher consciousness. From that moment on, this story would often surface within my mind to broaden my awareness and guide me. It has also become a periodic reminder of the nature of the way itself.

> A STREAM, from its source in far-off mountains, passing through every kind and description of countryside, at last reached the sands of the desert. Just as it had crossed every other barrier, the stream tried to cross this one, but it found that as fast as it ran into the sand, its waters disappeared.
>
> It was convinced, however, that its destiny was to cross this desert, and yet there was no way. Now a hidden voice, coming from the desert itself, whispered: 'The Wind crosses the desert, and so can the stream.'
>
> The stream objected that it was dashing itself against the sand, and only getting absorbed: That the wind could fly, and this was why it could cross a desert.
>
> 'By hurtling in your own accustomed way you cannot get across. You will either disappear or become a marsh. You must allow the wind to carry you over, to your destination.'

But how could this happen?

'By allowing yourself to be absorbed in the wind.'
This idea was not acceptable to the stream. After all, it had never been absorbed before. It did not want to lose its individuality. And, once having lost it, how was one to know that it could ever be regained?

'The wind', said the sand, 'performs this function. It takes up water, carries it over the desert, and then lets it fall again. Falling as rain, the water again becomes a river.'

'How can I know that this is true?'

'It is so, and if you do not believe it, you cannot become more than a quagmire, and even that could take many, many years; and it certainly is not the same as a stream.'
'But can I not remain the same stream that I am today?'

'You cannot in either case remain so,' the whisper said.

'Your essential part is carried away and forms a stream again. You are called what you are even today because you do not know which part of you is the essential one.'

When he heard this, certain echoes began to arise in the thoughts of the stream. Dimly, he remembered a state in which he -or some part of him, was it?–had been held in the arms of a wind. He also remembered -or did he?–that this was the real thing, not necessarily the obvious thing, to do.

And the stream raised his vapor into the welcoming arms of the wind, which gently and easily bore it upwards and along, letting it fall softly as soon as they reached the roof of a mountain, many, many miles away. And because he had had his doubts, the stream was able to remember and record more strongly in his mind the details of the experience. He reflected, 'Yes, now I have learned my true identity.'

The stream was learning. But the sands whispered: 'We know, because we see it happen day after day: and because we, the sands, extend from the riverside all the way to the mountain.'

And that is why it is said that the way in which the Stream of Life is to continue on its journey is written in the Sands. (Shah, 1970, p. 23-24)

On the Road with the Buddha

My experience of this notion of remembering the essential part of myself was deepened by my exposure to Buddhism. My first introduction to the Buddhist tradition was through the discourses and written works of Thich Nhat Hanh, a Vietnamese Zen Buddhist monk. I found his presence and words inspiring and I began doing some of the mindfulness practices he recommended. Through this process, I came to more fully understand that to connect with the Divine I needed to reconnect with my true self or essential part, and that the gateway to this self was emptiness, and that this gateway was reached by the stilling of all thought.

> Dispersed mind is also mind, just as waves rippling in water is also water. When mind has taken hold of mind, deluded mind becomes true mind. True mind is our real self, is the Buddha: the pure one-ness which cannot be cut up by the illusory divisions of separate selves, created by concepts and language. (Thich Nhat Hanh, 1976, p. 42)

As I continued to explore various forms of Buddhism, I felt both drawn to it and resistant. I would be guided to go to a book, practice, lecture, ceremony, or workshop. Then I would have a strange experience that would distance me from the material. These strange experiences often came in the form of an uncomfortable trance-like state of consciousness. One particular experience occurred at Esalen while I was attending a Tibetan Buddhist White Tara Ceremony.

The visiting monks began the ceremony by chanting. Their deep swirling voices blanketed the room and I suddenly felt physically and mentally exhausted. I struggled to keep my eyes open but finally fell into a deep trance state. This state seemed like a mixture of dream, deep sleep, and meditation all at once. All of a sudden I woke up and the ceremony was over. The memory of the experience was like a dream whose images float away like a drifting shadow on the edge of awareness. While I recognized that I had experienced a powerful altered state, I also felt awkward, confused, and very uncomfortable.

After this experience, and others like it, I distanced myself from Buddhism for a while. Then one day, I felt powerfully drawn to a course in Buddhism. My mind came up with various excuses not to take it, yet something within me was telling me I had to sign up for the class. The following week I was sitting in the classroom, listening to the discourse, while apprehensively waiting for the trance-state to appear. I was surprised when nothing happened.

That weekend I bravely opened up one of the assigned books, *The Tibetan Book of Living and Dying*,[92] and began to read. I connected deeply with the material and could not put it down. When I came to the section on the *phowa practice*,[93] a voice inside told me that I had to do this practice every day. I was apprehensive at first because this practice seemed to be geared toward death and dying, but my guidance was so strong that this apprehension quickly dissolved. As I read further, I learned that this practice was also used by the living as a way of cleansing the self in preparation for one's inevitable death.

I began to do the phowa practice several times a day, gradually memorizing its form. Slowly I discovered that this practice was deepening my ability to surrender to the Divine and access guidance. As I envisioned the embodiment of divine truth in the form of radiant light, repeated the phowa prayer, and imagined the Divine purifying me, I felt a powerful force within and around me.

> Through your blessing, grace, and guidance, through the power of the light that streams from you: May all my negative karma, destructive emotions, obscurations, and blockages be purified and removed, May I know myself forgiven for all the harm I may have thought and done, May I accomplish this profound practice of phowa, and die a good and peaceful death, And through the triumph of death, may I be able to benefit all other beings, living or dead. (Sogyal Rinpoche, 1992, p. 215)

I came to see clearly that "through this practice you are investing your mind in the wisdom mind of the Buddha or enlightened being, which is the same as surrendering your soul to the nature of God."[94] What I did not see at this time was the true gift and purpose of this practice.

Journey through the Valley of the Shadow of Death

It had been over a year since my healing and work-study retreat at Esalen. In that time I had declared bankruptcy, left the film business once again, and returned to school to study transpersonal psychology. I had found a new sense of purpose in my life and followed my guidance to places unimagined. The Sufi stories that penetrated me in my fall quarter class on Sufism and the Buddhist phowa practice I had learned in the Buddhism class I had taken in the winter quarter had become integrated into my spiritual life.

In the last quarter of my first year I had enrolled in a class on the spiritual dimensions of human behavior with anthropologist and Basque Shaman, Angeles Arrien. She spoke about an old tribal wisdom which says that you cannot reach enlightenment if you do not first honor and respect (re-examine) your family, religion, and culture of origin.[95] Her words penetrated my whole being and I had an inner knowing that this was the work I needed to do.

After class I began to reflect on my relationship with my family, religion, and culture of origin. I had left behind my religion of origin, Judaism, many years ago and never looked back. My thoughts about America were mostly critical or non-existent. Most of all, I realized that for the last several months I had been avoiding all contact with my family because I could not deal with the situation around my mother's debilitating condition and how this was tearing my family apart. That night I prayed for guidance and opened my eyes. I felt a strong force drawing my attention to the telephone. I had a deep inner prompting to pick up the phone and call my father. After a moment's hesitation, I picked up the phone and dialed the number.

My father picked up the phone and after a few awkward moments of conversation he told me that they had just made the decision to take Mom off life support. I told him I'd like to come and say good-bye to her. The next week my wife Sarah and I flew to Phoenix. We entered the Hospice and walked down the corridor past the chapel. There was a mural of Jesus on the wall. With each footstep I prayed. Entering the room, my mother's twisted and shriveled body laid motionless in the hospital bed before me. They had just taken out the tubes that were keeping her alive. The doctors said it might take two weeks for her to starve to death, but they would ease her pain with drugs. Her large dark brown eyes stared at the window even though her vision had darkened months before.

I sat quietly in the room with my wife, my father, my sisters, and my brother-in-law. There was a vast silence that filled the atmosphere. My mother could not see or speak or move her body, except for small motions of her hands, head, and feet. Automatically I started to perform the phowa practice for my mother within my heart and mind. Suddenly, tears streamed down my face as I realized the amazing set of circumstances that had prepared me for this moment. During the next few days I performed the phowa practice at her bedside repeatedly in my mind. I would picture the divine light above her, shinning down upon her, and transforming her being. The image of the divine light sometimes took the form of the Buddha, Jesus, or Abraham.

We all took turns sitting with my mother. Sometimes all of us were there, sometimes just a few, and sometimes just one of us alone. I remember the extreme sorrow I felt sitting by her side even though I believed in God and a life beyond this one. Her physical presence was drifting away and leaving me. After a while I would have to take a break and go outside and sit on the hospice patio. During one of these breaks I had a profound mystical experience. I walked outside after sitting by my mother's bedside for several hours. The April Phoenix sun was warm and bright. The desert flowers were in bloom and the warm dry air gently danced across my skin. As I sat outside on that patio, the beauty around me overwhelmed me. Each moment was crisp and sharp and so deeply alive. I found myself sitting between deep sorrow and profound beauty and every second filled me with its worth. I felt as though I was sitting amidst a sacred landscape.

When I returned to the room I continued the phowa practice. As I pictured Jesus over Mom's bed she slowly moved her head and looked up in the exact place I was envisioning him. For a brief moment her tense and twisted body melted into a relaxed state and I could feel a sense of peace fill the room. A while later the whole family sat in the room, swimming in the silence of sorrow and uncertainty once again. I felt guided to read from a book I had brought with me on the trip. I moved my chair close to my mother's bed and began to read from Stephen Mitchell's *The Enlightened Heart*,[96] an anthology of sacred poetry from the world's spiritual traditions. A miraculous change occurred and for the next few hours we all took turns reading sacred poems to my mother…and to ourselves.

> The Golden God, the Self, the immortal Swan
> leaves the small nest of the body,
> goes where He wants.
> He moves through the realm of dreams;
> makes numberless forms…
> But He is not attached to anything that He sees;
> and after He has wandered
> in the realms of dream and awakeness…
> He returns to the blissful state from which He began.
> - *Brihadaranyaka Upanishad, IV.3.12-22*[97]

On the night before Sarah and I had to leave, I went to the hospice to spend some time alone with my mother. I held her hand and assured her that I would be okay, and that she could move on. I also told her about my out of body experience, conveying my belief that the other side was real, and that she didn't need to be afraid. I told her I loved her and forgave her for everything, and asked for her to forgive me. I said good-bye with tears in my eyes. She squeezed my hand and, miraculously reaching beyond her physical inability to speak, she whispered: "Bye Mark."

Sarah and I returned to California. Two nights later I had a dream. Mom, Sarah, and I were climbing a rope ladder up into a helicopter. As the helicopter took off, I noticed that mom wasn't afraid. She was happy and light-hearted. I remembered how most of her life was spent in fear. She seemed so different now. We landed in a restaurant, and sat at a round table with the entire family. Mom ordered food without care or concern, which was again, so unlike her. She smiled, said good-bye, and left the table. I woke up. It was three in the morning. Sarah opened her eyes. She said she had a dream . . . it was the same dream as mine. The next morning my sister called to tell us Mom had died at three that morning. A shiver moved through me. I was deeply sad yet profoundly touched by her spirit.

One day later Sarah and I were on a plane for Chicago for the funeral. After taking off, I began to read a book about the Jewish grieving process that I had recently stumbled upon.[98] I looked up and saw the American eagle emblem on the seat back in front of me. Here I was flying home on American Airlines on my way to honor my family while studying Jewish spiritual practices. I felt enveloped by the tribal wisdom that had sent me on this sacred journey.

At the funeral I sensed an air of tension between our immediate family and my mother's family. As I walked toward the grave I entered a state of consciousness in which I perceived the yin-yang dance of the way of things that the Taoist tradition had taught me. I was aware of the feelings of separation around me and for the first time was able to just be with the conflicts of family. The boundaries of all things seemed to dissolve, as I felt moved to hug members of both families. I felt Mom's spirit around the coffin and my tears were flowing out of a sweet sorrow.

Toward the end of the burial ceremony, the Rabbi handed my father a bag of soil from the Holy Land. Each member of my immediate family sprinkled some of this Holy soil into Mom's grave. I was the last one to receive the soil. There was a lot left. My father and the Rabbi told me to pour it all in. I looked over and saw my mother's sister and brothers in tears. The inner voice whispered in my mind and guided me to pour a small portion of the soil into the grave and then motion to my mom's family to take part. I felt a great strength move through me as I handed the soil to my Aunt.

After the funeral I felt guided to perform the yearlong Jewish grieving rituals and practices, in honor of my mother's passing. Slowly, what had begun as an act of honoring my mother's memory became a journey of return to my religion of origin. The prayers penetrated my whole life in ways I had not imagined. They guided me through the valley of the shadow of death and into the bright sunlight of renewal.

> The Lord is my shepherd, I shall not want.
> He gives me repose in green meadows.
> He leads me beside the still waters to revive my spirit.
> He guides me on the right path, for that is His nature.
> Though I walk through the valley of the shadow of death,
> I fear no harm, for you are with me.
> Your staff and Your rod comfort me.
> You prepare a banquet for me
> in the presence of (all obstacles).
> You anoint my head with oil; my cup overflows.
> Surely goodness and kindness
> shall be my portion all the days of my life.
> And I shall dwell in the House of the Lord forever.
> *- Psalm 23*

My Return to Judaism

When I was growing up, my family's religious life was mostly a social experience. We would gather at home on Chanukah and Passover to perform the required rituals as quickly as possible, and then eat a lot of good food. We went to services only on the High Holy Days, and mumbled prayers in-between "kibitzing" with the neighbors. There were always a few old timers who actually seemed to be deep in prayer. They seemed to be in some other reality than the rest of us, as they mumbled the prayers at breakneck speed, lost in a deep and serious ecstasy while rhythmically rocking their bodies. I never really thought much about them until recently because, at the time, we were all caught in the game of looking down on each other ... the devout seemed to look down on us "one time a year Jews" and we laughed at their "backward" ways.

Between the ages of eight and thirteen, I attended Hebrew school to study and prepare for my Bar Mitzvah. The principal of the school was a man who had been tortured by the Nazi's in World War II. His inner pain, hatred, and anger manifested into verbal abuse toward the students who were not fully committed to the path. I was one of those students. I started to hate going to classes more and more each day. My belief in God was slowly eroded by a combination of the emotional abuse I experienced from the Hebrew school principal, the lack of spiritual experience in my family's religious life, and an inability to relate to a judgmental, war-like, jealous, and partial God. By the time I completed my Bar Mitzvah I had lost all connection to Judaism in my heart and mind.

Now, after many years of self-imposed exile and numerous experiences with many other paths, I found myself returning to Judaism ... or perhaps it was Judaism returning to me? As I began to practice the rituals of grieving in honor of my mother, I started to have my first mystical experiences on the Judaic path. These experiences grew out of a process in which I retranslated the traditional Jewish prayers into a language that resonated with my own heart. Later on I was to discover that this translation or exegetical process is in itself a form of Jewish spiritual practice.[99]

This exegetical practice began with a simple moment of guidance during one of my sessions performing the prayers for mourning. The inner voice softly told me to look up the original Hebrew words for the translated phrases that felt uncomfortable to me. To my surprise, as I explored the Hebrew dictionary and the traditional rabbinical teachings, I found that most Hebrew words have several different meanings, and can be translated in numerous ways. Additional meanings for every Hebrew word and letter were also to be found in the vast reservoir of the literature of the Jewish mystical tradition of Kabbalah. As I explored both the traditional and mystical sources, and applied some of these alternate meanings to the prayers, I was ushered into an unexpected and powerful transformational process.

After completing the year of mourning practices, I was gradually guided by the inner voice to create translations of the traditional morning, afternoon, and evening Jewish prayers, and put them into practice. This process evolved over the years, and became part of the methodology for my research into the experience of Divine guidance. I began this exegetical practice by reading the various translations of a given prayer while observing my reactions to the texts in order to discern areas of intuitive preference, disturbance, and discomfort. I would then explore these psycho-spiritual emotional issues through a focused meditation process. Once I gained clarity in relation to the areas of preference and discomfort, I searched the literature for deeper and alternative meanings of the words within these problem areas. Finally, with the aid of the intuitive and divine guidance processes I had learned over the years, I re-translated the prayers using these deeper and alternative meanings in combination with the translations of others. Once complete, I utilized the prayers in my daily practice.

Gradually I discovered that many of these alternative definitions and hidden meanings pointed to psycho-spiritual qualities of experience. As I used these psycho-spiritual definitions and meanings in place of the traditional words and phrases, all the disturbances and discomfort I had experienced around the traditional prayers disappeared.

The first major word that was transformed by this process was the word "Israel." Traditionally, this word is used as a label for the tribe of all Jews and as the name of the land that the tradition considers its sacred home. My exegetical inquiry uncovered that this word relates to the story in the book of Genesis of Jacob wrestling with the stranger from Heaven.[100] The various other meanings of the word Israel come from the essence of this teaching story: The one who wrestles or struggles with; one who yearns; the song of the Divine; and the Awakening Self. Once I replaced the word Israel with the phrase "the Awakening Self," a profound shift occurred for me. Suddenly the prayers were calling for my own growth and transformation, instead of reminding me of a separate people or place. Through this process, the prayer called the Shema was transformed from "Hear O Israel: The Lord is our God, the Lord is one"[101] to "Hear the Awakening Self: The Source of Life is the Fountain of all Being, the Source of Life is One."[102]

As I utilized these translations in my daily practice I began to experience deep mystical states and feelings of joy and peace. Gradually I realized that this process was helping me confront and heal my old wounds around the Jewish tradition. As I would confront and heal these wounds, I sensed that I was also being purged of some of the obstacles I had created between the Divine and myself.

> Stand at the crossroads and look,
> and ask for the ancient paths,
> where the good way lies;
> and walk in it,
> and find rest for your souls.
> - *Jeremiah 6:16*

Gradually, as I explored this territory, I began to get the sense that mysterious unseen forces were guiding me. Often I would receive guidance through what the Jewish tradition refers to as "the Speaking Silence."[103] My experience of this speaking silence was similar to that of hearing a voice whisper in your ear, except that all you experience is the reception of the idea being spoken. Sometimes I felt as though many different masters or teachers were communicating with me in this way. I soon discovered that as one enters the realm of Kabbalah, that the voice of God comes through the great teachers of the past who instruct you from within your mind and heart.[104]

> God acts within every moment
> and creates the world with each breath.
> He speaks from the center of the universe,
> in the silence beyond all thought.
> Mightier than the crash of a thunderstorm,
> mightier than the roar of the sea,
> is God's voice silently speaking
> in the depths of the listening heart.
> - *Psalm 93*[105]

Often, I would be guided by a series of signs that seemed to lead me to needed sources and experiences. One such episode occurred during my internship year of graduate school. I had been researching different Kabbalistic literature, trying to find a practice that resonated with me. By the end of the first semester I had reached a point of frustration, having not been able to find a Kabbalistic practice that felt right. I gave up my search and decided to enjoy the winter vacation time.

During the winter break the symbol of the tree seemed to invade every area of my life. First we bought a Christmas tree, and then the winter storms cracked open a tree in our yard. The next day our avocado tree started to bud for the first time. A week later we explored the redwood forest with visiting family members, and one of them bought a "tree of life" tee shirt. For Christmas I received a gift of an audio CD called *The Memory of Trees*,[106] and a friend of mine told me he was writing a song about the tree of life. The first week of the New Year I hit my head on a tree branch while walking to my car in a parking lot. Finally, a week before Tu Bhishvat, the Jewish New Year for the trees, I was in a bookstore and was mysteriously drawn to a book on Kabbalah that had a picture of the "tree of life" on the cover.

> Every day, God grants us signs,
> showing us the way of truth.
> - *Or Ha-Emet 2b*[107]

As I opened the book I realized that this was the answer to my yearning for a Kabalistic guidance practice. The book, *Miraculous Living*,[108] was a guided journey through the ten gates of the "Tree of Life" intended to bring one into more direct contact with divine guidance. The meditations and lessons beckoned the reader to "... attune your ears to hearing the voice of God in all sounds, and open your eyes to seeing wonders in many guises; look for the mystery behind the obvious and discern the truth beneath the veil of illusion."[109]

On the day following the New Year for the trees, I began to follow the practices in the book. The guidance practices I learned from this book strengthened my ability to access guidance and deepened my level of awareness during the guidance experience itself. Over the years I have gone through the book numerous times, and have incorporated its practices into my daily life.

> Show me one thing.
> Show it to me more clearly and deeply.
> Show me what this,
> which is happening at this very moment,
> means to me,
> what it demands of me
> - what you, Lord of the World,
> are telling me by way of it.
> - Rabbi Levi Yitzchak of Berditchev[110]

Throughout my journey of return to Judaism I also discovered many teachings on guidance that resonated with the other traditions I explored. Like so many of the other spiritual paths, Judaism beckons one to seek the Divine, to empty oneself of all that stands in the way of divine contact, to dwell in silence, to listen deeply, and to follow the guidance one receives.

> Emptiness is the first step in going within and touching God. When you empty your mind of clutter, your heart of expectations, and your body of excess stimulation, you become an empty vessel ready to receive God. Only if you are empty can you reflect God's image, echo God's voice, and be filled with God's light. Expectations, fear, confusion, and chaos leave no room for anything else. (Labowitz, 1996, p.35)

My barriers between Judaism and my self slowly dissolved as I re-discovered the tradition from a fresh perspective and saw the beauty that was always there, but somehow hidden to my eyes and heart. I discovered that the Judaic literature is filled with a strong belief that the Divine is always with us, and is continually offering us guidance and support, and a great promise of the blessings one will receive when following the guidance of the Divine.

> Call to me and I will answer you,
> and will tell you great and hidden things
> that you have not known.
> - *Jeremiah 33:3*

> Hear counsel, and receive instruction,
> that thou may be wise in the rest of thy life.
> - *Proverbs 19:20*

> By paths they have not known
> I will guide them.
> I will turn the darkness before them into light,
> the rough places into level ground.
> - *Isaiah 42:16*

> Adonai will guide you always...
> and you shall be like a watered garden,
> like a spring of water,
> whose waters never fail.
> - *Isaiah 58:11*

> Trust in the Lord with all your heart...
> In all your ways acknowledge him,
> and he will make straight your path.
> - *Proverbs 3:5-6*

Indeed, as I survey the whole of my experiences, I realize that my wayward journey and my return has been a great gift of divine guidance. My exploration of other traditions has given me a greater perspective of my religion of origin, and my return to Judaism has anchored my spiritual work, allowing the teachings of the other traditions to coalesce into a vision of the Divine that is more expansive and inclusive, and has deepened my ability to access the Divine.

This vision of the Divine was symbolized in a dream I had in the midst of my return to Judaism. I saw the symbols of many faiths spinning in a bright blue sky. One by one they attached themselves to each other. When they all connected to one another they turned transparent. They formed a large multifaceted crystalline structure. A white light filled the sky and its rays penetrated the crystal. Suddenly a brilliant rainbow rippled through the crystal and I saw the image of a face. I cannot say if the face was male or female, young or old, black or white . . . it was a faceless face, one of pure light.

> All sages of wisdom
> have one religion,
> they have one caste,
> they all behold
> the face of the One!
> - *Dadu*[111]

The Remembered Gate

Through my exploring and re-membering of my experiences of the Divine I have deepened my understanding of my experiences and my self. I continue to seek the Divine and its guidance in all my endeavors and persist in my efforts to incorporate divinity into my everyday life. At various times I have been able to connect with this experience of inner guidance through practice and through grace.

This guidance comes to me in many forms: Sometimes through an inner voice, dream, inner vision, or an intuitive feeling; sometimes I perceive receiving messages through external signs and synchronistic events; and sometimes I simply feel an energetic pull to move in a certain direction. I constantly struggle to discern the difference between divine guidance and my own internal dialogue, and attempt to align my words and actions with some of the qualities that seemed to be part of this divine communication. These qualities, as I sorted them out, included love, compassion, nonjudgment, and forgiveness.

My explorations into divine guidance have given me a taste of a state of being that feels intensely natural, as though it was my true or "original" state. When I am in this state of being, all of life seems to be held together by a gentle, loving gravitational force. The ultimate purpose of this spiritual autobiography has been to create a vehicle for my continuing exploration of this experience, to provide a means of self-reflection, and to offer a possible map of this mysterious and mystifying territory. And now, as I arrive at the end of this part of the journey, I am filled with a deep sense of gratitude and awe, and an abiding awareness that this is also the beginning…

With the drawing of this Love
and the voice of this Calling
We shall not cease from exploration
And the end of all our exploring
Will be to arrive where we started
And know the place for the first time.
Through the unknown, remembered gate
When the last of earth left to discover
Is that which was the beginning;
At the source of the longest river
The voice of the hidden waterfall
And the children of the apple tree
Not known, because not looked for
But heard, half heard, in the stillness
Between two waves of the sea.
- T. S. Elliot, "Little Gidding"

Notes

[1] Dunne, 1967, p. vii
[2] Fry, 1944, p. 145
[3] Erickson, 1998; Morgan, 1996; Wakefield, 1990
[4] Dunne, 1967
[5] Goldberg, 1991
[6] Alter, 1981; Dunne, 1967; Goldberg, 1991
[7] Ochs & Olitzky, 1997; Smith, 1983
[8] Underhill, 1961, p. 133
[9] Kaplan & Fienberg, 1985
[10] Csikszentmihalyi, 1990; 1993; 1997
[11] Csikszentmihalyi, 1993
[12] Ibid, p. xiii
[13] Kaplan & Hollander, 1974
[14] Kaplan, 1980
[15] *Oxford Dictionary and Thesaurus*, 1996
[16] Kaplan, 1981
[17] Kaplan & Lieberman, 1986
[18] Rilke, 1981, p. 13
[19] Storm, 1972, p.14
[20] Myerhoff, public lecture, September, 1979
[21] Myerhoff, public lecture, December 12, 1979
[22] Eliade, 1964
[23] Myerhoff, personal communication, December 12, 1979
[24] Castaneda, 1968

[25] Novak, 1994, p.369-370
[26] Ibid
[27] Kaplan & Fienberg, 1985
[28] Campbell, 1949; Castaneda, 1968; Harner, 1980; Jung, 1961; 1964; Storm, 1972
[29] Kaplan & Fienberg, 1985
[30] Ibid
[31] Eliade, 1964
[32] Kaplan & Fienberg, 1985
[33] Storm, 1972, p.371
[34] Deloria & Stoffle, 1998
[35] Novak, 1994, p.362-363
[36] Shaman's poem, Chukchee tribe of Siberia, adapted by David Cloutier (1973, p. 32-33)
[37] Mitchell, 2000, p.53
[38] Yogananda, 1983
[39] Kaplan & Fienberg, 1985
[40] Yogananda, 1983
[41] Self-Realization Fellowship, 1956
[42] Kaplan & Fienberg, 1985
[43] Patanjali, 1953
[44] Baba Hari Dass, 1981
[45] Bogart, 1997
[46] Baba Hari Dass, personal communication, July, 1986
[47] Ram Dass & Levine, 1976
[48] Ram Dass, public discourse, 1986
[49] Ram Dass, Public Discourse, 1991
[50] Ibid
[51] Underhill, 1961
[52] Bhagavad-Gita, 1904, 2:16
[53] Penington. 1863, II:4
[54] Hesse, 1968
[55] Ibid

[56] *Course in Miracles* (1996)
[57] *Bhagavad-Gita*, 1904, 2:16
[58] Hastings, 1991, p. 4
[59] *Course in Miracles*, 1996, Text, p. 398
[60] *Course in Miracles*, 1996, Workbook, p. 195
[61] Alschuler, 1993
[62] Ibid
[63] Shepard, 1991
[64] *Course in Miracles*, 1996, Text, p. 384
[65] *Course in Miracles*, 1996, Workbook, p. 382
[66] Williamson, 1987
[67] Kaplan, 1994
[68] Brother Lawrence, 1978; Merton, 1961; Steindl-Rast, 1984
[69] Mitchell, 1991, p.110
[70] Grof & Grof, 1990
[71] Ibid, p. 31
[72] Grof & Grof, 1989; 1990
[73] Grof & Grof, 1989
[74] Bragdon, 1990, p.1
[75] St. John of the Cross, 1990, p. 37
[76] Cox & Lopez, 1992
[77] Grof & Grof, 1990; St. John of the Cross, 1959; Underhill, 1961
[78] Fleming, 1983
[79] St. Ignatius, 1964
[80] Ibid, p.37
[81] Buckley, 1973
[82] Setzer, 1978
[83] St. John of the Cross, 1990; Underhill, 1961
[84] Bragdon, 1990; Grof & Grof, 1990
[85] Lao Tzu, 6, 1995
[86] Heider, 1985
[87] *Tao Te Ching*, 1972; 1988; 1995
[88] Dong & Esser, 1990; Liao, 1990; Liu, 1997; Yen-Ling, 1993
[89] Lao Tzu, 51, 1988

[90] Fadiman & Frager, 1997
[91] Shah, 1970
[92] Sogyal Rinpoche, 1992
[93] Ibid
[94] Ibid, p. 216
[95] Arrien, public lecture, Spring, 1993
[96] Mitchell, 1989
[97] Ibid, p.3
[98] Shapiro, 1986
[99] Fishbane, 1998
[100] Gordis, 1995
[101] Harlow, 1985, p.101
[102] Kaplan, 1999
[103] Ezekiel 1:4
[104] Halevi, 1979
[105] Mitchell, 1993, p. 42
[106] Enya, 1995
[107] Green & Holtz, 1977
[108] Labowitz, 1996
[109] Ibid, p. 153
[110] Ibid
[111] Quote by the sixteenth-century Indian saint-poet Dadu (Fox, 2000)

References

Dante Alighieri (1884). *The divine comedy* (Henry Wadsworth Longfellow, Trans.). Boston: Houghton, Mifflin, and Company.

Alschuler, A.S. (1987). Recognizing inner teachers: Inner voices throughout history. *Gnosis, 5,* 8-12.

Alschuler, A. S. (1993). Inner teachers and transcendent education. In K. Ramakrishna Rao (Ed.), *Cultivating consciousness: Enhancing human potential, wellness, and healing* (pp. 181-193). Westport, CT: Praeger Publishers/Greenwood Publishing.

Alter, R. (1981). *The art of biblical narrative.* New York: Basic Books.

Arrien, A. (1992). *The four-fold way: Walking the paths of the warrior, teacher, healer and visionary.* San Francisco: HarperSanFrancisco.

Baba Hari Dass (1977). *Silence speaks.* Santa Cruz, CA: Sri Rama Publishing.

Baba Hari Dass (1981). *Ashtanga Yoga primer.* Santa Cruz, CA: Sri Rama Publishing.

Baba Hari Dass (1986). *Fire without fuel.* Santa Cruz, CA: Sri Rama Publishing.

Bhagavad-Gita (Annie Besant, Trans.). (1904). London: Theosophical Publishing House.

Bhagavad-Gita: A new translation (Stephen Mitchell, Trans.). (2000). New York: Harmony Books.

Bogart, G. (1997). *The nine stages of spiritual apprenticeship: Understanding the student-teacher relationship.* Berkeley, CA: Dawn Mountain Press.

Bragdon, E. (1990). *The call of spiritual emergency: From personal crisis to personal transformation.* San Francisco: Harper & Row.

Buckley, M. (1973). Rules for the discernment of spirits. *The Way, 20,* 19-37.

Michelangelo Buonarroti (2003). *Brainyquotes.* [online]. Available: http://www.brainyquote.com/quotes/quotes/m/q100894.html.

Campbell, J. (1949). *The hero with a thousand faces.* Princeton, NJ: Princeton University

Castaneda, C. (1968). *The teachings of Don Juan: A Yaqui way of knowledge.* New York: Pocket Books

Cloutier, D. (1973). *Spirit, spirit: Shaman songs and incantations.* Providence, RI: Copper Beech Press.

Course in miracles. (1996). New York: Viking Penguin Books.

Cox, B. (Producer), & Lopez, T. (Writer-Director). (1992). *Chain of desire* [Film]. New York: Distant Horizons Productions.

Csikszentmihalyi, M. (1990). *Flow: The psychology of optimal experience.* New York: Harper & Row.

Csikszentmihalyi, M. (1993). *The evolving self: A psychology for the third millennium.* New York: HarperCollins Publishers.

Csikszentmihalyi, M. (1997). *Finding flow: The psychology of engagement with everyday life.* New York: HarperCollins Publishers.

Deloria, V. & Stoffle, R. W. (1998). *Native American sacred sites and the department of defense*. Washington, DC: United States Department of Defense [online]. Available: https://www.denix.osd.mil/denix/Public/ESPrograms/ Conservation/ Legacy/ Sacred/toc.html.

Dong, P. & Esser, A. (1990). *Chi gong: The ancient Chinese way to health*. New York: Paragon House.

Dunne, J. (1967). *A search for God in time and memory*. London: Macmillan.

Eliade, M. (1957). *The sacred & the profane: The nature of religion* (Willard R. Trask, Trans.). New York: Harcourt Brace Jovanovich.

Eliade, M. (1964). *Shamanism: Archaic techniques of ecstasy* (Willard R. Trask, Trans.). New York: Bollingen Foundation.

Elliot, T. S. (1999). *Little gidding* [online]. Available: http://www.sover.net/~bland/littlegi.htm.

Enja (1995). *The memory of trees* [CD]. New York: Reprise Records.

Erickson, C. (1998). *Arc of the arrow: Writing your spiritual autobiography*. New York: Pocket Books.

Fadiman, J., & Frager, R. (1997). *Essential Sufism*. San Francisco: HarperSanFrancisco.

Fleming, D. (Ed.). (1983). *Notes on the spiritual exercises of St. Ignatius of Loyola*. St. Louis, MO: Review for Religions.

Fishbane, M. (1998). *The exegetical imagination: On Jewish thought and theology*. Cambridge, MA: Harvard University Press.

Fox, M. (2000). *One river, many wells*. New York: Jeremy P. Tarcher.

Fry, J. M. (1944). *In downcast Germany*. London: J. Clarke & Company, Ltd.

Goldberg, M. (1981). *Theology and narrative: A critical introduction*. Philadelphia, PA: Trinity Press International.

Gordis, D. (1995). *God was not in the fire*. New York: Scribner.

Green, A. & Holtz, H. (1977). *Your word is fire*. Ramsey, NJ: Paulist Press.

Grof, S., & Grof, C. (1989). *Spiritual emergency: When personal transformation becomes a crisis*. Los Angeles: Jeremy P. Tarcher, Inc.

Grof, C., & Grof, S. (1990). *The stormy search for self: A guide to personal growth through transformational crisis*. Los Angeles: Jeremy P. Tarcher, Inc.

Halevi, Zeb ben Shimon (1979). *Kabbalah: Tradition of hidden knowledge*. New York: Thames and Hudson.

Harlow, J. (Ed.) (1985). *Siddur Sim Shalom: A prayerbook for Shabbat, festivals, and weekdays*. New York: The United Synagogue of America.

Harner, M. (1980). *The way of the shaman*. New York: Harper & Row

Hastings, A. (1991). *With the tongues of men and angels: a study of channeling*. Fort Worth, TX: Holt, Rinehart and Winston, Inc.

Heider, J. (1985). *The Tao of leadership*. Atlanta, GE: Humanics New Age.

Hesse, H. (1968). *Narcissus and Goldmund*. New York: Bantam Books.

Holy Bible, new King James version. (1979). New York: Thomas Nelson Publishers.

Hume, R. E. (Trans.) (1971). *The thirteen principal Upanishads*. London: Oxford University Press.

Saint Ignatius (1964). *The spiritual exercises of Saint Ignatius* (Anthony Mottola, Trans.). New York: Image Books.

Jalal al-Din Rumi (1940). *Mathnawi Manawi* (R.A. Nicholson, Trans.). London: Gibb Memorial Series.

Jalal al-Din Rumi (1984). *Open secret: Versions of Rumi* (J. Moyne & C. Barks, Trans.). Putney, VT: Threshold Books.

Saint John of the Cross (1990). *Dark night of the soul* (E. Allison Peers, Trans.). New York: Image Books.

Jung, C. G. (1961). *Memories, dreams and reflections* (R. & C. Winston, Trans.). New York: Vintage Books.

Kandinsky, W. (1977). *Concerning the spiritual in art*. New York: Dover Publications.

Kaplan, M. A. & Fienberg, G. (Producers), & Kaplan, M. A. (Writer-Director). (1985). *Voice in exile* [motion picture]. Los Angeles, CA: American Film Institute Center for Advanced Film Studies.

Kaplan, M. A. and Hollander, E. (1974). *Progress* [motion picture]. Chicago, IL: Chicago Board of Education.

Kaplan, M. A. and Lieberman, E. (1986). *Write This Down* [screenplay]. Los Angeles, CA: Original Gravity Productions.

Kaplan, M. A. (Writer-Director-Editor). (1980). *Gun* [motion picture]. Los Angeles, CA: University of Southern California School of Cinematic Arts.

Kaplan, M. A. (Writer-Director-Editor). (1981). *Write this down* [motion picture]. Los Angeles, CA: American Film Institute Center for Advanced Film Studies.

Kaplan, M. A. (1994). *The ark of consciousness: A creative inquiry into spatial design* [Master's Thesis]. Palo Alto, CA: Institute of Transpersonal Psychology.

Kaplan, M. A. (1999). *Prayers for the awakening self - the daily cycle: A psycho-spiritual siddur for weekday practices*. Pacific Grove, CA: Original Gravity Press.

Kaplan, M. A. (2005). The experience of divine guidance: A qualitative study of the human endeavor to seek, receive, and follow guidance from a perceived divine source. *Dissertation Abstracts International, 66* (05), 2855 (2005). (UMI No. 3174544)

Kings (A. Cohen, Trans. & Ed.). New York: The Soncino Press.

Krishnamurti, J. (1969). *Freedom from the known*. New York: Harper & Row.

Labowitz, S. (1996). *Miraculous living: A guided journey in Kabbalah through the ten gates of the tree of life*. New York: Simon & Schuster.

Lame Deer, J., & Erdoes, R. (1972). *Lame Deer, seeker of visions*. New York: Washington Press Square Press.

Lao-tzu (1972). *Tao te ching* (Gia-fu Feng & J. English, Trans.). New York: Vintage.

Lao-tzu (1988). *Tao te ching* (Stephen Mitchell, Trans.). New York: Harper & Row.

Lao-tzu (1995). *Tao de ching* (Peter Merel, Trans.) [online]. Available: http://www.chinapage.com/gnl.html.

Brother Lawrence of the Resurrection (1978). *The practice of the presence of God* (Sister Mary David, Trans.). New York: Paulist Press.

Liao, W. (1990). *T'ai Chi Classics*. Boston: Shambhala.

Liu, H. (1997). *Mastering miracles: The healing art of Qi gong as taught by a master.* New York: Warner Books.

Merton, T. (1961). *New seeds of contemplation.* New York: New Directions Publishing.

Mitchell, S. (Ed.). (1989). *The enlightened heart: An anthology of sacred poetry.* New York: Harper & Row.

Mitchell, S. (1991). *The gospel according to Jesus: A new translation and guide to his essential teachings for believers and unbelievers.* New York: HarperCollins.

Mitchell, S. (1993). *A book of psalms.* New York: HarperCollins.

Mitchell, S. (1998). *The essence of wisdom: Words from the masters to illuminate the spiritual path.* New York: Broadway Books.

Mitchell, S. (2000). *Bhagavad-Gita: A new translation.* New York: Harmony Books.

Morgan, R. L. (1996). *Remembering your story: A guide to spiritual autobiography.* Nashville, TN: Upper Room Books.

Myerhoff, B. (1976). Balancing between worlds: The shaman's calling. *Parabola, 1(2),* 6-13.

Novak, P. (1994). *The world's wisdom.* San Francisco: HarperSanFrancisco.

Ochs, C. & Olitzky, K. M. (1997). *Jewish spiritual guidance: Finding our way to God.* San Francisco: Jossey-Bass Publishers.

Oxford dictionary and thesaurus. (1996). New York: Oxford University Press.

Patanjali (1953). *How to know God: The Yoga aphorisms of Patanjali* (Swami Prabhavananda and Christopher Isherwood, Trans.). New York: Mentor Books.

Penington, I. (1863). *Works of Isaac Penington, vol. 2*. Glenside, PA: Quaker Heritage Press.

Ram Dass & Levine, S. (1976). *Grist for the mill*. Berkeley, CA: Celestial Arts.

Rilke, R.M. (1981). *Selected poems of Rainer-Maria Rilke* (Robert Bly, Trans.). New York: Harper and Row.

Rodin, A. (2003). *Brainyquotes*. [online]. Available: http://www.brainyquote.com/quotes/quotes/a/q132246.html.

Self-Realization Fellowship (1956). *Self-realization fellowship lessons* (Volume 1). Los Angeles: Self-Realization Fellowship.

Setzer, J. S. (1978). How can I determine when it is God who speaks to me in my inner experiences? *Journal of Pastoral Counseling, 12*, 41-54.

Shah, I. (1970). *Tales of the Dervishes: Teaching-stories of the Sufi masters over the past thousand years*. New York: E. P. Dutton.

Shapiro, R. M. (1986). *Open hands: A Jewish guide to dying, death and bereavement*. Miami, FL: Temple Beth Or

Shapiro, R. M. (1989). *Unhewn stones: A high holy day mahzor*. Miami, FL: Temple Beth Or.

Shepard, L. A. (Ed.). (1991). *Encyclopedia of occultism and parapsychology* (3rd Ed.). Detroit, MI: Gale Research, Inc.

Smith, H. F. (1983). Discernment of spirits. In D. L. Fleming (Ed.), *Notes on the spiritual exercises of St. Ignatius of Loyola* (pp. 226-248). St. Louis, MO: Review for Religious.

Sogyal Rinpoche (1992). *The Tibetan book of living and dying.* San Francisco: HarperSanFrancisco.

Steindl-Rast, Brother David (1984). *Gratefulness, the heart of prayer: An approach to life in fullness.* New York: Paulist Press.

Storm, H. (1972). *Seven arrows.* New York: Ballantine Books.

Thich Nhat Hanh (1976). *The miracle of mindfulness.* Boston: Beacon Press.

Underhill, E. (1961). *Mysticism: A study in the nature and development of man's spiritual consciousness.* New York: E. P. Dutton & Company.

Wakefield, D. (1990). *The story of your life: Writing a spiritual autobiography.* Boston: Beacon Press.

Williamson, M. (Speaker). (1987). *Marianne Williamson on a course in miracles: Keeping it light* (Cassette Recording No. 082-042187). Los Angeles, CA: Marianne Williamson.

Williamson, M. (1994). *Illuminata: Thoughts, prayers, rites of passage.* New York: Random House.

Yen-Ling, S. (1993). *Tai Chi Chuan: The basic exercises.* Tokyo: Sugawara Martial Arts.

Yogananda, Paramahansa (1957). *How you can talk with God.* Los Angeles: Self-Realization Fellowship.

Yogananda, Paramahansa (1983). *Autobiography of a Yogi.* Los Angeles: Self-Realization Fellowship.

Made in the USA
Las Vegas, NV
11 February 2021